7/1/06
Marilyn Raphael
Sheree Wu

ANGELIC FORCE

A Modern Medium's
Communication
with the Spirit World

Marilyn Raphael
Sheree Wu and Victor K. Chu, PhD

DoubleLight Publishing, Inc.

MILPITAS, CALIFORNIA

DoubleLight Publishing, Inc.
PO Box 361935, Milpitas, California 95036-1935
www.doublelight.com

The techniques described in this book are not meant to replace formal medical or psychiatric treatment. Individuals with medical problems should consult their physicians for advice and appropriate treatment. The intent of the authors is to offer information of a general nature to help readers improve their emotional and spiritual well-being. The authors and the publisher make no warranty as to the appropriateness of the techniques described herein to treat specific conditions. Readers who make use of information contained in this book do so at their own risk.

Library of Congress Control Number: 2005935635
ISBN-13: 978-0-9773602-0-8
ISBN-10: 0-9773602-0-2

Printed in Canada
on acid-free, 100% recycled paper

10 09 08 07 06   1 2 3 4 5

For James and Eileen, my Angelic Force;
my mother, Sadie, my Eternal Beacon;
my daughters Felicia and Jane,
with whom I share boundless love;
my grandson, Jeffrey,
who shines like a star and is the darling of my life;
and the sweetest new addition to our family,
my granddaughter, Elizabeth, whose smile melts us all.
–M.R.

For my father, Thwen-Shinn Wu (吳存信),
who taught me integrity, ethics, and love;
and for my mother, Su-Yuan Lee (李蘇元),
who grew with me in the realm of understanding spirit
communication.
–S.W.

For my mother, Sally Ching-Hsueh Chu (林慶雪),
who always stands by me,
and for my father, Henry Hsing-Pang Chu (朱興邦),
who knows how to appreciate life.
–V.K.C.

Contents

Acknowledgments

Many mortal and spirit entities contributed to this book. It is impossible to name them all, but deep gratitude goes out to each and every one of them.

Without the angelic force of my beloved spirit entities who purport to be that of James (Ya'akov bar Yosef) and Eileen J. Garrett, this book would not exist. For more than forty years the entity James has brought into my life others from his spirit realm, teachers from whom I have learned, grown, and shared. They include Ernest Miller Hemingway; June, a wise Chinese medicine lady who may have been the ancient spirit of Abdul Latif, who worked from the spirit realm with Eileen when she was mortal; and so many others.

Among the many mortals who have stood by me through difficult times and put themselves at risk of being labeled "different" or "suffering from delusions," my enormous thanks go to:

Doris Lipetz, a dear friend and confidante from Brooklyn Heights, New York, who stood by me during the early stages of the deeper trance states. She has been ever supportive and allowed me to conduct classes in her home at a time when this subject matter was not freely spoken of and considered a taboo. She gave me endless private time to question and explore this phenomenon. Her friendship and kindness will forever remain special in my life.

Rita Rudow, who is a joy to be with and brings merriment to all we do together. She is a loyal friend whom I take along on most of my adventures that involve haunted houses, séances, classes, and research.

Sharon McConnell, a dear friend who for several years took on the task of organizing and overseeing much of my work. She steadfastly continues to motivate and encourage me regardless of whatever obstacles are present.

My warmest and most appreciative thanks go to a very special and gifted young lady who has been with me since her arrival into this world. Jane is not only my daughter, she is also my confidante and friend, and has currently taken on the enormous task of managing my affairs as they relate to this work.

Warm thanks go to my dear friend Sanda Gane, who has blessed my life in so many positive ways, always with love, generosity, and encouragement.

My thanks also go to a rare and a special friend, Su-Yuan Lee, who I know shared a life in the spirit realm with me.

—Marilyn Raphael

We would like to thank those people who shared their readings and experiences, no matter if they choose to reveal their true identity or to be anonymous.

Our thanks, then, to: Karen Goldberg, Zoraida Navarro, Joyce Oates, Tracey Richmond, David and Janet Rosenzweig, and Alaine Sorkin.

Hearty thanks go to Doris and Joel Hochheiser for their hospitality during our visit to Florida in December 2004. Also thanks to Doris for kindly inviting us to observe her club's platform reading with Marilyn, and for her efforts on obtaining the permission from all the people mentioned in her stories in Appendix C.

Thanks to Don DeHart, Fritz Krieger, Sylvia Sun Minnick, and Roslyn Parker for listening to our story and generously providing positive suggestions.

Thanks to Professor Liwei Lin of the University of California at Berkeley for assisting our research regarding Chinese medicine women.

Thanks to our editor, Meghann French, who treated our whole book like her own baby. She provided both gentle care and strong discipline. She was persistent yet not imposing. She not only fully understood our writing but also frequently asked pertinent questions that helped us write clearly. We admire her professional knowledge and appreciate her pure kindness.

Thanks also to Stella Panos for her work in transcribing taped interviews. We would not have been able to document these stories without her work.

Thanks to Laura Adriaan and Jennifer Wong for their time and efforts in proofreading our book. We treasure their graciousness and friendship very much.

Thanks go to Ingrid Chen, Jessie Chen, Nancy Dai, Daphne Lin, Lei Hsu, and Yi Sun for being excellent listeners during the lengthy process of writing this book. The love from these empathetic friends motivates us to continue marching on the challenging and exciting journey. They also helped us realize our own psychic ability. We all grew together on the spiritual path, becoming more aware of our potential and enjoying practicing telepathy with each other.

Special thanks go to all of our family members, including but not limited to Kelly Chu, Anita Kuo, Charles Wu, Richard Wu, and Catherine Su, who patiently provided morale support throughout the writing process.

Thanks to all other friends who have been patiently waiting for the completion of this book.

Last but not least, we want to thank all the spirits that helped us write this book. Without the spirits' help, we could not have walked this far. It is our huge honor to present the true stories and help the readers understand the spirit communication.

—Sheree Wu and Victor K. Chu

The three of us would like to thank Martin Ebon for his time and effort on writing a foreword to this book. It is our honor to have a foreword from Martin, a gentleman of exquisite charm, passion, wit, and intelligence, with a full understanding about the work of a medium. During the process of writing this book, Martin made himself available for generous consultation. His uncanny timing regarding when to telephone, offering hope and good advice, is immeasurable.

Foreword

I Call Her "Unique"

Martin Ebon

Although psychic sensitives are numerous, divided into different categories, and have been applying their gifts for thousands of years, Marilyn Raphael's talents are unique. Today we refer to such people alternately as "mediums," "channelers," "intuitives," simply as "psychics," or, to make doubly sure, as "psychic mediums." Their skills, specialties, credentials, and reputations vary greatly. Individuals calling themselves psychics can be found on side streets in major cities, while others promote their services by telephone. Often, their practices and skills do not meet ethical standards, although it would be irresponsible to generalize negatively with regard to their talents or effectiveness.

Historically, mediumship has mainly been associated with communications linking us to dimensions beyond bodily death, with entities who exist on a higher plane of spiritual development. Previous generations tended to refer to these entities exclusively as "spirits," and to contact with this next world as "Spiritualism." Oddly, this latter term has become associated—largely by fictional accounts of practices going back to the Victorian age—with darkened rooms, an atmosphere ranging from fascination to dread, and emotional risks, such as spirit possession.

Regrettably, much of religious and dramatic tradition has given prominence to such practices as exorcism, all too often dramatized in fantastic horror stories and in crudely exploitative television shows and motion pictures. If we study early accounts of such phenomena, we find that only fear-inspiring tales have been passed down to us—precisely *because* they had the most disturbing emotional impact.

In my research, I have encountered a heartbreaking case of apparent spirit possession from thousands of years ago. A clay tablet, found in the temple of Asurbanipal, a powerful ruler of ancient Babylon, contains the desperate plea of a man who feels persecuted by an evil spirit. He appeals to three gods— Ea, Shamash, and Marduk—to free him from this possessing ghost. He pleads that the persecuting spirit be controlled in the netherworld, and chained, *with bolt and bar*, so that it can never again torture a living being, physically or mentally.

Today, if such a case were brought to the attention of a medium of the quality and experience of Marilyn Raphael, she would respond by teaching her client to deal with the troubling spirit, using simple human courtesy, listening to the spirit and urging it to free itself from its earthbound state, move on to a dimension better suited to its position, and seek the company of more mature guiding entities. Spiritualists have long formed healing circles specifically designed to guide earthbound spirits toward a suitable spiritual level; because Marilyn believes, contrary to the view passed down from our Victorian forebears, that troublesome spirits are simply confused rather than malicious, she might ask a qualified psychiatrist, working in tandem with her mediumistic insight, to contribute the services at the command of contemporary psychotherapy to assist a particularly troubled individual.

As a sophisticated twenty-first-century medium, Marilyn Raphael has pointed out to me that the tasks she faces—such as sensing the psychic and/or psychotherapeutic needs of people encountering inexplicable experiences—go well beyond spiritistic traditions. At the historic outset of our modern fascination with mediumistic sittings, pure curiosity and even entertainment were major motivations. During the second half of the nineteenth century, as well as during and after World War I, séances were common. At the same time, genuine mediumship was imitated by stage magicians and irresponsible charlatans. (Even today, magazines serving professional magicians advertise ingenious tricks designed to imitate legitimate mediumistic practices.)

Mediumship is a rare, delicate, and even elusive talent. Books with catchy titles such as *Mental Radio* and *Telephone between Two Worlds* convey the false impression that it is possible to contact the dear departed at will. All of our existence, all of our worldview, would be a great deal more serene, peaceful, and mutually tolerant if someone like Marilyn could simply *call the spirits* as quickly and reliably as envisioned by authors and playwrights, including William Shakespeare. Often, spirits refer to a medium as "the instrument," but even that more enlightened terminology fails to fully acknowledge the delicate role a medium plays.

Entities can be exasperatingly elusive, talking in code or confusing metaphors. They have minds of their own, and we must make allowances for their own frustrations in trying to communicate with us. This difficulty in communication can lead to irritation on both sides, as when one group of entities endorses the concept of reincarnation and another denies it—possibly in convoluted, elusive terminology. And why do we often get a choice of first names, and have difficulty eliciting a family name? But then, of course, we sometimes do get both, the first time around.

Marilyn is eminently admirable. Like so many psychics, she had trouble as a child understanding how to best develop her gifts in the face of a culture that had been conditioned to regard them with suspicion and fear. She learned early on that she could not always be completely candid with others—even those closest to her—about her experiences, and faced a great challenge in maintaining a degree of separation between her everyday life and her interaction with the spirit world. She even began to question her own sanity, living as she did in a world that was not yet prepared to accept her experiences as quite "normal."

And as if all of us did not have enough trouble with family, friends, and other people we encounter in our everyday lives pulling our energy and attention in different directions and adding their own two cents to the paths our lives take, Marilyn's spirit friends often added another dimension to the challenge. In helping her to explore and develop her talents, they often nudged her in a particular direction with regard to the mundane choices of everyday life. In a manner evocative of the fact that these spirits were once *human*, they lent their personal tastes to influence her choices in style of dress, social interactions, and other day-to-day decisions—and sometimes the suggestions of one stood in direct contrast to another's.

With characteristic strength and wit, however, Marilyn managed to rise above the challenges presented by her gifts, meeting obstacles head-on and learning how her talents could best be used as a force for good. Over the years she has shared her gift with others: bringing messages from the spirit world to those living in the human plane, teaching scores of students how to develop their own psychic potential, and bringing peace to those dealing with troublesome spirits. And somewhere along the way, the public at large began to regard psychic phenomena with more curiosity than fear. Some might say this is to Marilyn's benefit; after a childhood and youth in which she felt she had to hide a part of herself from those who might not understand, she now lives in a world prepared to accept her gifts without fear. But it is equally possible that it is precisely because Marilyn—and other ethical, responsible mediums like her—has spent her career presenting the spirit world and psychic communication with it as phenomena to be celebrated, not feared, that this tide has turned.

There is a vast gap between an ethical mediumistic professional such as Marilyn Raphael and high-priced star performers we encounter on television talk shows. An anomaly in our commercial society, Marilyn respects grief and mourning to the degree that she refuses to accept payment from clients who come to her in a state of bereavement. And in this era of hype, she had to be cajoled into permitting this autobiography to see the light of day. Those of us who feel that the responsible middle ground of mediumship—between those who dismiss all claims out of hand and the dubious telephone psychics and performers who purport to have psychic abilities—needs to be better understood can be persuasive to the point of badgering. To elaborate on a well-known psalm: "There is a time to keep quiet, and there is a time to badger!"

Very well, then! Read on!

New York
December 2005

In his half century as an active researcher and author in psychic studies, Martin Ebon lectured at academic institutes throughout the world. He served as administrative secretary of the Parapsychology Foundation in New York City, where he worked with Eileen J. Garrett, then president of the foundation, for twelve years. He was the author or editor of more than eighty books, including They Knew the Unknown, Prophecy in Our Time, *and* Psychic Warfare: Threat or Illusion? *He also prepared research reports for the Institute for Borderlines of Psychology and Mental Hygiene in Freiburg, Germany. Mr. Ebon passed away in February 2006.*

Prologue

Unscheduled Flight

Sheree Wu

Two days before the Christmas in 2002, I called Marilyn Raphael for the first time. I was calling on behalf of a client, whom my husband, Dr. Victor K. Chu, and I met at an international hypnotherapy conference. I was trying to strike a business deal among several parties. At that time Victor and I knew little about Marilyn. Marilyn, who lived about three thousand miles away, knew absolutely nothing about us.

Soon after our conversation started, I realized that my client might have withheld some information and that the deal was more complicated than I expected. Marilyn was quite upset about the behavior of my client's practice. Not knowing the history between Marilyn and my client, I just listened quietly for two hours without taking sides. After the business conversation was over, I politely said good-bye to Marilyn and was ready to hang up.

"Wait a second," Marilyn said.

"What?"

"You are petite," she said.

I was surprised and asked, "How do you know?"

I could hear her smile in her voice as she replied, "Don't forget that I am a psychic."

Then Marilyn opened up and said many things about us. She said that we had just bought a house and we had rented an apartment earlier. She said that we had just started a small proprietary business. I told her that the name of the company was DoubleLight. She understood the meaning immediately and said, "Of course. You are a light and your husband is a light."

Marilyn continued, "You or your husband is very good at computers." I told her that it was Victor. Although Marilyn didn't know it, he was working in front of a computer at that very moment. Marilyn then said, "He is an engineer . . . a pro-grammer." Then she said that we would have relatives visit us the following February. It was true that both my mother and my father-in-law were planning to visit us in February. Marilyn even told me that one of our cars needed to have its tires rotated.[1]

Victor and I were very impressed by the quality of the infor-mation that Marilyn revealed. Chinese fortune-tellers usually need to ask your birth date and hour so that they can do some calculations and then say something about you. Marilyn did not ask any of our personal information, yet she was able to say so much about us over the phone. And what Marilyn was about to say was even more amazing.

---

[1] Initially, I did not follow Marilyn's suggestion on rotating the tires. We had two cars, so we didn't know which car Marilyn was talking about. Victor visually inspected the tires and didn't find anything wrong. Three months later, when Marilyn gave me a personal reading, she brought up this topic again. She asked, "White Toyota, whose car is it?"

"I have Victor's mother here," Marilyn said.

My mother-in-law had passed away fourteen months earlier. Marilyn could not have known this. She said that Victor's mother would visit us that night and we would sense the smell of flowers. After my mother-in-law passed away, my sister-in-law Kelly had sensed the smell of roses several times when there were no flowers around, so I found Marilyn's comment interesting. But I was not convinced that the message was really from my mother-in-law.

Marilyn continued, "I've got your father here."

I did not believe what I heard, since Marilyn had never heard of me before that day. Neither did she know that my father had passed away three years earlier. I joked with Marilyn, "Yeah? So what does my father want you to tell me?"

"Your father wants you to tell Su that he loves her very much."

Su (蘇) is the first character of my mother's Chinese name, Su-Yuan (蘇元). My grandfather was a general in Chiang Kai-shek's army, and my grandmother chose the character Su because my grandfather's troops were stationed in Suzhou (蘇州) at the time of my mother's birth. Hearing my mother's name coming from a complete stranger's mouth made me speechless. Very few people in the United States knew my mother's name. After my father passed away, my mother rarely interacted with people outside the family circle. Even in Taiwan, my mother had been known as Mrs. Wu or Professor Lee, as Chinese usually don't address their elders by their given names.

Marilyn continued, saying, "You have a Joe here?"

"Living or dead?" I asked.

"Deceased. A spirit. Your father is telling me that you have a Joe nearby."

"No, I cannot think of anybody named Joe who is deceased," I said.

"No," said Marilyn, "Not Joe. Jiu4 [falling tone of Jiu] ... Jiu2 [rising tone of Jiu] ... Jiu3 [dipping tone of Jiu] ... Jiu3-Jui2 ... Jiu4-Jiu4 ... Jiu4-Jiu [neutral tone of Jiu] ... Jiu4-Jiu!"

It seemed as though Marilyn was mimicking the sounds of a language that was totally foreign to her. She corrected herself several times to match the exact tone of a Chinese word. I realized that Marilyn had just successfully imitated the pronunciation of Jiu4-Jiu (舅舅), which means "maternal uncle" in Chinese. Indeed, my mother's oldest brother suddenly passed away in Taiwan in 1989 at the age of fifty-five. My grandmother and my other uncles all lived in the United States at that time. It was my father who arranged the funeral for this uncle.

I was stunned. Marilyn then broke the silence and asked, "Could you write a book for me? You can write my stories."

I thought Marilyn must be joking because she had never seen any of my writing. I answered, "Well, of course it will be an honor for us. But don't you want to see my writing first? I can send—"

She interrupted me. "You can send whatever you'd like to send. I am sure they are well written. I just want you to write my stories."

That was how we boarded our unscheduled flight. We collected some of her notes, drawings, pictures, audiotapes, and transcripts of trance sessions. We also started conducting our own phone interviews with Marilyn. Twice a week, she told us about her life stories and we recorded our conversations on tape. We followed up in the next interview on issues that were not clearly addressed. We gathered as much as we could of her stories, philosophy, and teachings. In the meantime, we talked to her friends, students, and clients so as to understand Marilyn from different points of view. We decided that most of this book is deliberately narrated by Marilyn so that the main tone is coherent for our readers.

≥⦿ ≥⦿ ≥⦿

We spent more than three years writing this book. During these years, we ran into miscellaneous obstacles frequently. Sometimes we were frustrated that the project did not progress as smoothly as we wished. Sometimes Victor and I felt that our points could not get across. Whenever I was in dire need for help and I did not know which mortal to turn to, I usually ended up with genuinely sending mental messages to the spirits for their help. Then, within a short period of time, we were surprised to find that the issues we had been worried about were completely resolved or not important anymore. Sometimes the questions which needed to be answered were correctly answered. Sometimes total strangers suddenly showed up to kindly help us remove the difficulties.

This kind of phenomena happened so often that Victor and I decided to document the messages I sent. We established special e-mail accounts for different spirits. E-mail messages sent to those accounts would be directed to my own in-box. Right after I sent the mental messages to the spirits for help, I typed the exact same messages to the appropriate e-mail addresses. Then we waited to see what would happen. Since the first time we started documenting my own communication with the spirit world, I have sent seventy-four messages to the spirit world. And they were all answered in time.

Victor and I are grateful that we are working with the angelic force to present the stories of spirit communication. The more experiments we did, the more fascinated we became. We also started to understand why Marilyn tells people, "Always use the willing exercise in a positive way." The spirits do hear us and respond to us.

⋅ ⋅ ⋅

Before we first spoke with Marilyn, we had never thought of writing a book with a world-class medium. During the process of writing this book, we were sometimes asked by various people, "Why did Marilyn choose you to work with? Why didn't she pick somebody else?" And in fact, Marilyn had been approached by many good writers who wanted to write about her stories. She declined all of them.

Later on, Marilyn said to me, "When you called, I felt the light and it continued growing. I felt that I have been waiting for somebody for a long time. And you finally showed up." In another phone conversation, she said, "We have met before." I asked her what she meant, but she didn't reveal more. On another day she said, "I feel that I have unfinished business with you."

Perhaps writing this book was not really an unscheduled flight for us. Instead, it might have been a flight scheduled a long time ago, even before this lifetime. Working with Marilyn has been an exciting journey for us. Marilyn leads us to understand the wonders of the spirit realm with a healthy, positive, and open attitude, and we would like to share our discovery with our readers.

Welcome aboard!

1

It Started with Grandpa

For thou art my lamp oh Lord, and the Lord will light my darkness.

—2 Samuel 22:29

ONE CHILLY SPRING morning in the late 1940s, I awoke from a dream in which my grandfather was speaking to me.

He said, "Tell Mommy I'm OK."

Not having an understanding of what dreams and messages from them meant, I told my mother, "I saw Grandpa and he told me to tell you he is OK."

My mother asked me what I was talking about. I said, "Grandpa came to me while I was sleeping. I was sitting in a rowboat. Grandpa Samuel was standing on the river's edge and was waving and yelling to me to give this message to you."

My mother said, "Don't be silly."

A day later, my mother got the news that her father had passed away the previous night.

Lessons and Love

Grandpa Samuel was a tall, thin, well-groomed man with a magnificent full head of white hair and a perfect white mustache to match. His soft, masculine features fit perfectly upon his handsome face. I had a healthy respect for him, and was somewhat in awe of him. He exuded charm and elegance and had a special charisma that made him glow whenever he walked into a room. His presence was charged with energy. He commanded respect and attention from others without ever having to utter a word.

My grandparents lived more than fifteen blocks away from our house. Grandpa suffered from severe diabetes and walked with a cane, yet this never stopped him from visiting us, and he managed the distance through both good and very nasty weather in spite of the pain he endured.

I was always very excited when he visited because I knew he would take me on long, slow walks. He could not walk without making many stops, and he was apologetic for doing so. I was in my glory just to be around him, so it mattered only that we spent time together. During the rest periods he explained to me about nature, pointing out the beauty of a single flower struggling to survive through the cracks in the concrete sidewalk, or explaining how a tree got its nourishment from the raindrops and morning dew left on its leaves. He brought his thinking and words to a level that I could comprehend.

In his own unique way, he taught me to love and respect the beauty that Mother Nature bestows upon us. My grandfather made the slums of Brooklyn feel and look like the Garden of Eden.

He always took my hand when we went for our walks, and he encouraged me to hunt for oddly shaped stones and bottle caps from the old green Coke bottles. The city streets became a treasure island. Once we'd brought all the loot home, I would spend hours cleaning and polishing my treasures before pasting them on paper to make little designs.

My endearing grandfather inspired me at the early age of four to appreciate and love nature and art.

He never said, "I love you," or anything mushy. He never held me in his arms to hug or kiss me, yet I felt very much loved.

When my mother was very ill and close to death, it was my grandfather who came and got me. He explained that we were going for a very long walk. We walked at a slow pace for more than thirty blocks to get to the hospital where my mother was. Since children were not allowed in the hospital, he showed me where to stand so my mother could stand at her hospital room window and wave to me, and I waited while he went inside to visit her.

When he returned, he struggled to lift me so I would have a clear view of her. I remember crying and waving like mad, throwing hundreds kisses at her and begging him to get me inside that hospital so I could be with her. I never wanted to leave that spot, but after a while we had to go because the weather was changing. It was very cold and windy, and now it was starting to snow.

He orchestrated that whole day just so I could see my mom, even though he could barely walk because his leg pain was horrific. We somehow made it back to his house, where my grandmother had hot soup ready for us.

During my mother's illness, my dad had to go to work and could not leave me alone. So I lived with my grandparents while my brother, who is four years older than I am, was allowed to remain home with my father. I stayed with my grandparents for many months until my mother recuperated.

Dream Visitors

When my mom was comfortable enough to question me about my dream, I told her in my childish way how he came and stayed until I got the message. My mother's reaction was one of disbelief, but this time she did not call me silly and she started to question me further.

Then I told my mother about other people who were visiting me, people I did not know. She spoke in gentle but firm tones, telling me that it was not a good idea to allow this to happen and expressing concern over what she considered to be too vivid an imagination.

I tried to explain how these people came to me in my sleep with brief messages to deliver to my mom. Sometimes it would be a neighbor, relative, or acquaintance, and they all said, "Tell your mom I'm OK" or "We are absolutely fine here."

My mom began to take note of the occurrences because most of the information I gave to her was correct. After a while she began to tell me to take little naps and report to her any information I gathered in my dreams. I got used to the greetings from these strangers who had passed away, and in all cases, these were people my mom had known at various points in her life. It happened so often that it began to seem ordinary. Imagine this happening to you at a very young age. I gave no thought to the idea that not everyone experienced so.

I did not know it then, but having to remember the people and their messages so I could report back to my mom laid a very good foundation for exploring and experimenting with the dream states that occurred many years later. So my mother unknowingly gave me a great gift.

Keeping Secrets

During my childhood, my mother, my grandmother, and I were the only people who were aware of the information that came through my dreams. I was forbidden by my mother to ever discuss this in front of my father, because, as my mother put it, he would never understand. I was one of those kids who always obeyed their parents, so when my mother said not to do something, I listened.

Keeping this secret from my father was sometimes difficult, but I knew my mother would protect me as best as she could, and if she felt it unwise to speak of this, then so be it. This was my first introduction to keeping a secret.

My father's family had come from Germany in the late nineteenth century. His family was traditional and no-nonsense. Looking back I can easily understand that my mother's decision not to tell him about the dreams was key to keeping harmony and peace in our family. This was definitely not a subject that was openly discussed in the 1940s, and if it had been, given my father's very stern attitude toward things, it might have been cause to consider me more than just odd.

Even though my father was a practical and logical man, he did have a soft spot in him. I remember how he used to try to make Christmas a fun event, filled with fantasy and mystery.

One Christmas Eve my father took a big cowbell and pretended to be Santa Claus. He shook the bell and I remember saying, "Oh! Thank you, God. Santa Claus is coming." I got down on my knees and prayed that Santa's sleigh could fit on the fire escape, since we did not have a chimney for him to enter through.

Although I yearned for a doll, I always got spin tops from Santa, and I remember telling my parents that Santa did not listen to me. They responded with gentle words, explaining how fortunate I was to even be on his long list when so many other children were not. True appreciation for love and kindness was the greater lesson.

Hearts of Gold

My parents were very loving people who concerned themselves with helping others who were a lot poorer than we were. Unlike many in my field, I had a happy childhood.

I did not understand what having little money and being poor meant, and I did not know that my parents had to give up something dear to them in order to give my brother and me a Christmas gift. My parents had their own way of teaching my brother and me virtues.

One day when I was about eleven years old, my pal Margaret (who was a year older and who I considered wiser than I) said, "I have horrible news to tell you about your family and mine and all of the people we know." She went on to say, "We are dirt poor and considered among the poorest and the lowest socioeconomic status in the world. My teacher said we are like garbage."

To my eleven-year-old brain, it was only the word "garbage" that got to me. It conjured up visions of bad-smelling things with bugs and rats crawling all over. Would I be put into a garbage pail, too, or burned in the backyard like the rubbish? Margaret and I were terrified of being garbage and we had an awful day dealing with that news.

Shocked by Margaret's words, I marched over to my mother and repeated the whole story. My mother's jaw dropped, and she said, "I will speak to your father about this."

I asked her to hurry, because I did not want to be disposed of like garbage.

After a while my parents had a very heartwarming and sensible conversation with me. It was my father who said, "Don't worry, we are not garbage. We are only money poor."

He pointed to his heart and asked me to do the same, and went on to explain how rich we were because we had hearts filled with love and compassion for mankind. We also had books to read that took us on journeys into other parts of the world.

Thus, he gently embraced the situation and managed to make us all feel better. He never failed to amaze me. For a man who was boss in his family and ruled it with a strict hand, he was also very generous and kind toward everyone, regardless of their circumstances in life.

Satisfied with my father's words, I told Margaret that we were not poor, because we had hearts of gold. She too was put at ease.

Mother Superior

It was during these tender years that I began to have a recurring dream two or three times a week. In this vivid dream I was running in the catacombs, calling after a mother who wore a long, brown nun's habit. I never caught up with her, and whenever I awoke from this dream my face was wet with tears.

She certainly was not my earthbound mother from this lifetime. One day I must have been crying very loudly, because my earthbound mom woke me up and cradled me in her arms, saying soothing things to calm me down. I looked at her and said, "I want my other mommy, the one in the tunnel." Eventually, my mother's gentle touch was enough to lull me back to sleep. This particular dream stayed with me well into my adult life.

Years later, I met the lady who I instinctively knew was the nun from the dream. It happened in the early 1990s. I was dining with my friend Rita, who wanted me to meet her friend, a well-known medium from Florida. From the moment that dear lady entered the restaurant, we both knew we shared a special bond from another time.

During that first meeting, our eyes locked as I began to share my nun dream with her. I told her I thought she was the Mother Superior from a different lifetime and it was she I was running after in the catacombs, calling out, "Mommy! Mommy!"

As she looked at me, her eyes welled up with tears, and mine did, too. We touched hands and held each other for a few brief moments, and then spoke passionately of our past shared life. She was able to relate to it completely and shared with me that she too was certain she and I had this very special connection from another life. She used to dream of being a Mother Superior. She also said the color of the habit was definitely brown. And we both think it was somewhere in Germany. We commiserated and spoke of our obligations and rituals, and how I grew up to be a nun in that lifetime, too.

The brief time we shared was rewarding to both of us. With deep respect and joy in our hearts, we both humbly went our separate ways, ever knowing that we had shared a common existence. I never had my nun dream again, and I believe we were meant to meet and share in our common knowing of the past.

Interestingly enough, Beverly is a full-trance medium in this lifetime. It is amazing to me that in our current existence, we still shadow each other's lives in a positive way.

Informative Dreams

Between the ages of eight and nine, my informative dreams began to taper off, and it remained so till I was twelve. At that point in my life, before puberty, the dreams began to connect in a way that allowed me to sense or be aware of events yet to be. Then the transfer of this awareness started to happen when I was awake as well.

It was during these light altered states of consciousness, somewhat like a daydream, that I could see my dreams as if watching a movie unfold.

I remember one day I envisioned our supper. In those days, my mother was doing her best to keep a balanced diet for us so that we did not lack any nutrition, so she had a fixed menu for each day of the week. On a day not scheduled for liver—which I till this day still cannot tolerate—in my mind's eye I saw my mother, wearing an apron embroidered with roosters, serving us liver. Later that afternoon, when I actually saw my mother put on the same apron I had seen in my dream, I knew I was in trouble, but I had a plan of escape. I kept my dog, Snooky, close by my feet, sneakily put the cut pieces of liver in my hand, and fed them to her under the table. My mother caught me doing this, and I was punished for wasting food. But I was happy that I skipped the liver!

At times I envisioned soldiers without legs. Then one day, not long after these visions, some friends of my father's who were Korean War veterans were invited to our house. Their trousers looked empty where a leg was supposed to be, and two of these men walked with crutches.

After our company left, my father explained how they lost their legs in the service of war. I wanted to share my dream with him, but I remembered my mother's caution about telling him anything regarding my dreams. I kept silent, but found it a curious thing that my visions included the living as well as the dead.

.   I also remember picking up on a few baseball games and seeing who would win. The information was correct. I was also sometimes told about the weather for the next day, or which relative might stop by for a chat with my mother. My mother did not know what to do with me; once again she was dealing with unknown territory. The word "psychic" was not a familiar one to my family or to me, and nothing that would have remotely touched upon the subject of the paranormal was part of my parents' daily lives.

Looking back on those years, I can imagine that my mother and grandmother must have thought me quite an oddity. But both adjusted their lives to accommodate mine. They did everything they could, in a quiet and graceful manner, to make me feel very normal. They did not make fun of what I said would happen. They did not brag about it, either. They knew there was something different about me, but they did not want me to seem strange to other children, our neighbors, or our family. They made sure that I had good manners and that I acted in a way that would be properly accepted. They shielded me from harm while secretly encouraging me to explore the odd thing that was happening to me.

Even though these events happened frequently, I grew up in a normal, healthy environment established by my parents. My parents were generous and their home was known as an open house for anyone who was hungry or needed shelter from the cold. People did not even have to knock; they would just walk right in. Whatever food was in the old icebox or the cupboard was set upon a huge oak table, so any guests who came to their home were sure to feel welcome.

It was during these preteen years that my ability to see what are commonly referred to as ghosts became apparent. I did not know that others could not see what I saw. Once again, my mother and grandmother had to handle a secret. The ghosts I saw appeared very much the same as you and I. The only difference was that they could disappear and walk through walls. I simply accepted them for what they were. I did not fear these entities; it was simply an occurrence that I became accustomed to.

Some of the ghosts that showed up were neighbors who looked somewhat familiar. The ghosts did not speak. I think I noticed them more than they did me because I remember saying hello or good-bye, but I do not recall them responding in kind.

One day I decided to follow a ghost who entered my building. Foolishly, I walked smack into a brick wall and got a bruise on my nose and chin. I never did that again.

As I approached my twelfth birthday, it became apparent that the informative dreams had just about stopped, and the beautiful ghostly manifestations came few and far between. This all happened slowly, and so it seemed the old door closed quietly and gently as a new one opened loudly.

New Doors Open

With the closing of the old door, and the loss of my dreams and ghosts, I felt a great loss. However, this was a short-lived sadness, mainly because something different was happening to me. A new awareness, taking place on the conscious level, was emerging, and floods of information entered directly into my thoughts. I began to simply *know* things.

Holidays with my family were the hardest—and sometimes the funniest. I could pick up what other members of the family were thinking. One day my favorite aunt was praising my mother for the wonderful feast she had prepared, endlessly complimenting her, but the message my mind picked up was quite the opposite.

I was young and ill equipped to handle this sort of thing. How was a twelve-year-old girl supposed to tell people that she knew they were lying, or that she knew their personal thoughts? It was especially difficult when dealing with adults. As a result, I learned early on to share these things only with Grandma and Mom, and I never let anyone else know. What was happening at that time was very different from my earlier experiences, and I did not know how to process the information appropriately. It became an awkward responsibility and, at best, a struggle to understand.

I felt very lost in this new territory. I tried very hard to ignore what I sensed about people, and in the early stages of this awareness, I cringed at receiving that sort of information. In time I learned to harness my emotions.

Keeping my knowledge hidden from others was sometimes a big challenge. My mother and grandmother had impressed their advice so strongly that I became fearful of the shame I could bring to my family. During the 1940s, 1950s and early 1960s, someone like me would have been misunderstood, made fun of, and ostracized. Although my mother and grandmother did their best to allow my abilities to develop, they made it clear in no uncertain terms that I was never to share any of this with others. I believed them when they said people would hurt me—and my family, for harboring a strange child like myself.

My Geiger Counter

Around the age of sixteen, grappling with this new awareness became second nature to me. It was strange in many ways.

Some of the information coming through was startling in its accuracy, while some wasn't. During these years I began to understand that my body was interacting in some way with information that came to me. When an unhappy event was to take place, I would feel a sensation in the area of my solar plexus and my stomach would jump. Sometimes, a gentle vibration would stay with me until the event finally occurred. Then I would go back to normal.

I recall an incident that occurred on a foggy, wet, rainy day when I was fifteen or sixteen. As bedtime approached, great sadness gripped me. I felt gloomy and could not sleep. My stomach was jumping. The usual remedies one takes for an upset stomach could not quiet it down. Several hours later, when my stomach suddenly quieted down, I knew that whatever was going to happen was in progress.

A few days later I found out that American Airlines flight 320 had crashed into the East River. Two crew members and sixty-three passengers died in that accident.

After experiencing my body's reaction to other shocking yet-to-be events, I learned that when my solar plexus reacts in a jumping or vibrating manner, it is an indicator that something is about to happen that may not be pleasant. So I call my solar plexus my Geiger counter. Throughout my life it has simply reacted by jumping, letting me know it is detecting an impending disaster.

Sensing Spirits

During this phase in my life another interesting phenomenon began occurring. Although I hardly saw my old friends the ghosts, I began sensing what I believe to be spirits.

Spirits are quite different from ghosts. Ghosts manifest themselves in a form resembling their mortal state. Ghosts do not do much except walk around. They tend to mind their own business and seldom communicate verbally. When I was young, I thought everybody saw ghosts and I did not make a fuss about it.

The sensing of spirits is much more intense than the seeing of ghosts. Different things would take place in my body, allowing me to sense, feel, and know that other entities were around. For example, I would hear messages in my head—or, more precisely, in the front of my head, just above and between the eyebrows. I got a tingling feeling and sensed a spirit. Or the corner of my mouth would droop or tighten when a spirit was near. For me it was a pleasant feeling, and I had lots of fun picking up on the personality of whatever spirit was nearby. As I grew accustomed to sensing them, it became easier to pick up on their thoughts, and this new interaction was exciting.

Astral Traveling

We all experience astral travel, and sometimes we are blessed with memorable adventures.

A new type of adventure arose in conjunction with spirit sensing. After I went to sleep, I would experience the sensation of rising out of my body. It started with a gentle vibration all over my body and then became a loud buzzing sound in my ears, like a roaring train. I would float up above myself and catch a glimpse of my sleeping body lying snugly in bed. Sometimes, I would fly very far above myself out of the house, rising up toward the clouds.

These traveling experiences occurred just a few times during my teenage years and did not return until many years later. As a teenager, I paid no heed to it because I believed it was a special part of a dream that all people have and are sometimes fortunate to remember.

I went on journeys, mostly all over New York City. I did not have control over where I would wind up, but I do recall some sweet memories from some of those trips. When I found myself in the homes of the people I knew, I would think to myself: "Everyone is sleeping. Time to leave and get home to my bed." No sooner did I have that thought than I would be returned to my bed. One time I visited my friend whose dog slept with her, and the dog looked at me as if it was aware I was there. Since I was not invited, I left.

I did not know what to do with this new form of adventure, and it sometimes embarrassed me to just pop in as an uninvited guest in the wee hours of the morning while everyone was sleeping. I felt uncomfortable and, although I was thankful to the spirits for this new experience, I asked for it to be taken away.

Shortly after that request, this type of journey stopped, and I thought my experience with these amazing feats was ended. Many years later, after I read about out-of-body experiences and astral travel, I pleaded with the spirits to give them back to me. The gift of these experiences was wasted on my youth, and it would be a long time before I was in a position to grow from the experience so I could teach it to and share it with others.

2

Automatic Writing

As the body without spirit is dead, so faith without work is dead also.

—James 2:26

As TIME WENT on, life began to get very busy. I was dating, working, and thinking of the future, which to me meant marriage and family. My ghost and spirit experiences seemed to be fading away, and I started to feel that I was no different from other people. So when I met my husband-to-be, I chose not to reveal the special experiences that had been part of my youth.

I didn't think that divulging the experiences, which I believed had gone to sleep for a while, would serve our new relationship well. After all, he was a man of science and needed concrete proof of things. We married in the early 1960s and I continued to keep this one secret to myself. I sincerely felt I was using good common sense.

I thoroughly enjoyed my life and was very content being a wife and hoped to be a mother soon. When my first child was born, I had little time for anything other than the occasional intuition that all mothers feel, or a spontaneous revelation through a dream. I felt the experiences of my youth were part of a closed chapter of my life.

Awakening

Things did not remain so simple and normal, however. I had not anticipated that the phenomenon of my youth would resurface after remaining dormant for several years, but it came one night with a gigantic bang and incredible force. I was awakened and literally pushed off my bed to the floor by unseen hands. My body ached slightly from head to toe. The area of my heart was especially tingling with what felt like an electric shock. I thought I was having a heart attack.

I was not scared, but I was very curious about what might be happening to me. A flood of old thoughts began to swim in my mind. I knew that something or someone wanted my full attention and chose this dramatic way of getting it. The events of my youth were being reawakened. I did not expect them to return with such a dramatic force, but I realized that I had to pay attention.

The unseen force disappeared and the aches in my body dissipated. Everything seemed to go back to normal. But I had no desire to sleep anymore. Instead, I walked into the living room and sat on my couch, waiting for the next *whatever* to take place. I stayed awake that whole night, waiting and waiting and waiting. Nothing happened. No one came to say hello. I then thought perhaps it was only a dream, and I admonished myself for being silly and allowing my thoughts to think that my past was coming back.

Nothing else happened that night or the next, or the one after that, so I felt comfort in believing that my past involvement with the spirit realm was still a secret.

Back then I did not know what the word "medium" meant. I knew only that in my youth I had seen ghosts and had been able to sense spirits and pick up information from them. If someone had told me that one day I would be communicating on behalf of many spirits, I would have considered him silly. And I did not want to be involved with the so-called dead. It was difficult enough just dealing with the living.

Fear of my secret eventually getting out made me bring the subject up with my husband. While I attempted to speak to this very logical man about such things, I was seized by fear and panic. When I tried to explain it to him, my tongue and mind were not able to perform in sync and the words I used were very confusing. I thought I sounded like a babbling fool. I knew that if I continued, he would think I was crazy, so I stopped my first attempt at this conversation. I promised that one day in the future, when I became better at explaining these things, I would provide a more intelligent, logical, and knowledgeable presentation.

My new difficulty in life was that as the experiences from my youth were coming back, there was no one to share them with. My friends in those days were not open to the paranormal, and I made it a closed issue with my family. I felt alone with both my new and old responsibilities. Meanwhile, remembering the exciting and thrilling adventures that had taken place in the past, I began to anticipate a new awakening. I was curious how I was going to juggle being a wife and mother and keep my paranormal studies a secret while finding space and time to research. I was in awe of the entity that had in my teenage years taken me on journeys during the simple and brief OBEs and astral travels, and hoped this gentle spirit was the one who would be my teacher, guiding me on the path of learning, growing, and sharing.

A week after the episode in which I was tossed off the bed, another interesting episode occurred. I was reading a book on my couch, in that state just before falling asleep where you are only slightly aware of things around you. I remember glancing at the clock, which read 2 AM.

I sensed someone unseen, very close to me. This feeling came with such a strong force that I had severe shakes and pain all over my body. I was unable to sit on the couch and rolled onto the floor. It felt like a million electric shocks, with pins and needles going through my entire body. I could hardly breathe and I thought I would certainly die this time.

The next thing I knew, I started to rise out of my body. I looked down at my somewhat twisted figure lying on the floor. Feelings of joy and peace overcame me. It was as if I had no body but a remembrance of one, so I no longer felt any pain. I kept going up and out of my building, toward the clouds. I was completely absorbed by the white clouds. The sensation of floating upward was so soothing and calming that I wished I could stay in that state forever. Then I felt a man's hand holding mine. This time there was a voice attached to it.

I was told by this strong force that he was my control entity and he would be with me for my entire life in this. He showed me my whole life up to that point. He spoke about being my teacher and my master, and said that one day, when he felt I was ready, he would bring a wise lady to teach me further. He would bring in the teachings from the spirit world for me to learn and grow from, to share and become enriched by.

His voice sounded like it was coming through a tunnel, resonating with a slight echo. He said I had much to learn and share with others, and most of all to fulfill my promise to become a medium for him and a lady whom I was yet to meet, and as a voice for other spirits who must connect to their living families.

He led me back to my house and told me to return to my body. It had felt so good to be out of the body that was still lying on the floor. I remember thinking, "Oh, I don't want to go back to that." At that moment my only thought was not of the survival of my mortal self, but of experiencing more of this complete calmness and the feeling of being embraced by a tremendous sea of love. But the next thing I knew, I was being pushed back into my body. I Immediately felt the excruciating pain again, but it did not last for long. When I came to, I looked up at the clock. It was 5 AM. I had been somewhere else for three whole hours, but it felt just like minutes. I had no sense of time or how much of it had passed. I was completely overwhelmed by this experience, and it is still as vivid in my mind as if it just occurred.

Later in my life, long after the episode, I learned that the control entity—control, for short—of a medium is a spirit entity that controls which spirits come through and which do not.

Many years later, I was told by my control entity, and by the wise female spirit he had sent to me, that in order for spirits to enter the domain of a mortal, one of the things that they must do is to pierce the veil. The veil, or aura, is an energy field that extends from each of us and goes for great distances away from our bodies. This may have been what happened on those two occasions when I found myself writhing in pain from what felt like electrical shocks to my body. Once the veil is pierced, it can never be closed. Now my aura is co-joined by my control entity.

For some mediums, there is a side effect with a pierced aura: whatever health issues they have may become magnified. In my case, my weak lungs became weaker and my fast heart rate became faster. One day Eileen, the wise female spirit my control entity had told me about, jokingly said that my spirit friends have invisible bandages in my body to keep it together. I am not sure I laughed at their comfort.

The night when I again met my control entity was a critical point in my life. After that experience, I became a physical medium, or a physical channeler, to use the modern term. This means that certain spirits, with the permission of my control, can come through me and use part of my physical body directly. They can use my voice directly and talk in their own languages, or they can use my hand to write.

A Twenty-Five-Year Lesson

One day, while I was writing a letter to a friend, my pen took off as if guided by unseen hands, making giant swirls and circles on the paper. I did not know what was happening to my hand. I took a fresh sheet and waited to see if my hand would do it again. Nothing happened. So I continued writing. This time I was able to finish my letter quickly—at least so I thought. But when I read the letter, I was astonished to see that much of it did not seem to come from me. Not only that, I did not have any memory of what I had written until I read it. When I looked at the clock, I saw that more than an hour had passed. Once again, I had experienced a loss of time for which I could not account.

This was very exciting since it appeared that another way of communicating with spirits was beginning to unfold. I decided to explore this new communication. I could not do it during the day because of the chores I had to attend to as a wife and mother. I disciplined myself to work on it each night from 2 to 4 AM. I chose this time frame because the rest of my family would be sleeping, so it allowed me the freedom to explore this new phenomenon.

Sitting at my kitchen counter with pad and pen, I was eager to start. In the early stages of this exploration, I thought I would simply put myself in a receptive frame of mind and then I would see the pen take off on its own accord, just the way it did the very first time. But that is not the way it happened. Instead, I found I did not know how it started, but I would awaken from an altered state and find I'd filled a page or two with writing.

This means of communication, I learned later, is called automatic writing. Automatic writing can be done with pen and paper or with other equipment, such as a typewriter, a computer keyboard, and so on. It usually happens when a person is in an altered state of mind, which is a slightly conscious state, or, for some, while in a full trance. At the beginning, all of my automatic writings were carried out with pen and paper during a deeper trance state. My writings can be roughly grouped into several categories, including economics, medicine, politics, and family.

Sometimes there were diagrams showing Earth and nearby planets. On one of those sheets, the writing indicated that a name would be given to a newly discovered planet in our solar system around the year 2000. This planet has always been there, but there were no telescopes powerful enough to pick it up.

In this altered state, I also wrote words in foreign languages. One day I woke up from an automatic-writing session to find a whole page of what looked like Asian or Hebraic letters. Upon checking them out, I realized that the message was for a lady in my neighborhood. It was a greeting from the spirit of her grandmother, who wrote, "Hello, and I love you" in Chinese. I should mention that I do not speak or write Chinese or any other foreign language.

Some of the automatic writings pertained to my own family members and their health issues. One particular writing was a diagram of the human body. Next to it was my father's name. Several parallel lines were drawn on the paper with one end pointing to the lungs. At the other end of these lines were the words: "Crumbles like an old sponge." I did not tell my father about this drawing because I was still keeping my involvement with the paranormal hidden from him, and even if he had known, I certainly would have spared him from being frightened by the news. In any event, I did not fully understand the implication of this diagram at that time. Several years later my father was diagnosed with lung cancer. The doctor told me that my father's lungs were like old sponges and crumbled to the touch.

Delusional or Not

This type of writing went on for a few months, and time eluded me every time the writing occurred. I was aware only of sitting at the counter and being ready to start, then later awakening to find messages that I knew did not come from me. Although I was enjoying the adventure, I had no one to share this with. A more frightening aspect of it was the need to make sure I was healthy in mind. I was still a very young woman, in my twenties, and there was not a day that went by that I did not question if I was losing my mind. So, seeking answers, I started to read books by Sigmund Freud, Carl Jung, and others.

I kept myself busy poring through psychology books. The more I read, the more scared I became. Sometimes I felt I was definitely sick. And worse yet, I felt that many of the symptoms described in the books applied to me. Delusion was high on that list. This caused me to take a break from my beloved work, which lasted for about three months.

I was becoming worn out from my desperate research. I was very afraid that I was having a mental breakdown, yet my daily life appeared normal and was full of activities related to my roles as mother, wife, and homemaker. I thought I experienced this partly because I was overloaded and not getting enough sleep, and partly because I was holding on to a secret existence. So I stopped reading psychology books and stopped questioning my sanity. I also started to do some new activities, such as drawing, in order to help me relax.

During my drawing sessions, my hand began to gently vibrate and once again take off on its own. I had to face up to what was happening. This time I promised to never again allow myself to become my own worst enemy. I prayed that the angelic force would understand my dilemma and begin to teach me again.

I did not have to wait long; we started right where we left off. But now I was fully conscious and in control of my hands while my control entity and sometimes other spirits gave me information to write down. Sometimes they would put me in a slightly altered state so they could write, too. Our handwriting was different. I am right-handed, and some of those who wrote through me had a slant to their letters that led me to believe they were left-handed. While this was easier on my nervous system, I had not yet stopped questioning my sanity. Although I was eager to work with the spirits, I felt I needed proof that the writing was coming from them.

One day my husband drove me to the bank so I could cash a check. It was a freezing day and my husband did not feel like getting out of the car, so I went into the bank alone. To my surprise, the manager of the bank refused to cash the check because my signature did not match the original on file. I looked around the bank to find help and spotted a neighbor who could vouch for my identity. I quickly called him over and asked him to say that he knew me. I could not believe what happened next. Instead of identifying me as Marilyn Raphael, my neighbor said, "I have no idea who this lady is."

I was stunned. I stood there with tears in my eyes and worried about my husband, who was waiting outside in the car. He thought this chore would only take a few minutes. I did not drive a car in those days, so I did not have a picture ID card to prove my identity. I calmed down a little bit and looked at how I signed my name on the check. It was definitely different. This finding embarrassed me, and I realized that I must have signed the check in an altered state.

So I begged, "Please give me another chance." I explained to the manager that my hands were frozen and that was why my signature looked different.

And in my head, I was yelling at the spirits: "OK, OK. I believe. I believe."

The manager of the bank finally gave me another chance. This time my signature passed without any problem. I was glad to have the check cashed.

When I asked the spirits why they did this to me, I was told it was because I was struggling so hard with the subject of my sanity. They wanted to prove to me that someone with authority in the area of handwriting would surely put to rest the question of whether I was delusional or going insane. It did, and I was very touched by what they had done on my behalf. I realized that what I felt, saw, and heard really came from the spirits. As I look back now, years later, I am amused at their way of showing me that they were around and they could gently affect my life in a positive way.

When I met my neighbor again, I asked him why he had pulled such a stunt on me in the bank. He said it tickled him silly to see me trying to prove my identity and he needed a good laugh, even if it was at my expense. I found it difficult to share in the joke, though.

≈ ≈ ≈

From the late 1960s to the early 1990s, I made sure that I finished all the work I had to do for the family by midnight. Then I would take a very light nap. After a while I did not need an alarm clock to wake me up for the automatic-writing exercise; my biorhythm just knew it was time to wake up.

I kept my 2-to-4 AM automatic-writing schedule faithfully for twenty-five years. Then one night I woke up to attend to my automatic writing, but nothing happened. I felt in my body that something was different. I had trouble with my throat, but I did not have a cold. I was not sick, either. I instinctively knew that this was going to end; I would not sit down and do this anymore. I was crushed because automatic writing had become a habit. I cried because it felt like losing a very dear and close friend.

But while one door was closing, others were opened. My other instincts were becoming much sharper and my visions were increasing. I was still writing, but information was coming to me in another manner.

James, a Brother of Yeshua

By the time I stopped automatic writing, I had long known the identity of my control entity. He started telling the sitters in séances in the early 1980s that his name is Ya'akov bar Yosef. He is a brother of Yeshua; Ya'akov is his Hebrew name. Sometimes he also uses his English name, James, and this is how we will address him.

I can sense my control entity when he is near me. There

is a smell of myrrh associated with him. I always sense him behind me, his opened arms protecting me. But he has never materialized himself in front of me, nor does he project his image in my mind. In actuality, I have never seen this persona.

Nevertheless, I do have a sense of how he may have looked in the mortal life that he associates with the most. I sense that he had a brown face and he stood between four feet eight inches to five feet tall. He had a lot of hair on his head— wild, like Einstein's—and hair around his mouth, like a beard. One cheek was a little higher than the other. I sense that he had big eyes, lines on his face, and wounds on his hands. He had a slightly deformed body; one hand was broken and gnarled, perhaps left disabled by beatings or an accident. He wore sandals or coarse material wrapped around his feet. As for his clothes, I feel he wore something like a potato sack with a heavy cord tied on it just below his waist. One day I sat down and said to him, "Please let me draw a picture of you. Let me just get your head to see if it matches what I believe you might look like." He did not object to that idea.

Over a couple of years, I spent hours and hours drawing many different pictures, and he told me that each of them was just a shade of him. So I tried to make a composite. One day I finished a picture with the caption: "James reincarnated in the 1800s as priest" (see Figure 2.1).

Sometimes I entered a slight trance state and wrote questions for James to answer. Sometimes the entity gave me advice on my daily life. For example, one day I was angry. That night during my automatic writing, I sketched a clown. James told me that I was doodling away the negativity, and he told me to finish the drawing so we could focus on more positive thoughts (see Figure 2.2).

James sometimes came through to talk with people in my

Figure 2.1: James reincarted in the 1800s as a priest.

Figure 2.2: Marilyn in doodling.

classes or during séances. At the beginning, he was not easily understood since he talked in archaic Latin. Then he talked in Old English, but still, nobody understood him. He learned modern English by watching TV and listening to the radio with me, and by picking up words from my conversations. The whole process took him many years, but his English has improved a lot, even though it is not perfect yet. He still loves to talk in ancient Aramaic sometimes.

James has had many lifetimes. His talk is mostly focused on his lifetime as Ya'akov. He says that he had a brother named Yeshua; his father was called Yosef, and his mother Miriam. They were Orthodox Hebrews and belonged to a sect called the Essenes. The Essenes were considered the holiest of the Hebrew sects; they worshiped God and studied the Kabala. James and his family were among the most devout of the sect's followers.

James followed Yeshua and witnessed many miracles that his brother performed. He has written documents about his brother, and these documents were buried in the caves of Qumran.[1] He said that one day his work would be unearthed.

James always ended his talk by a chanting in ancient Aramaic: "Yee-Ya-Na,[2] Yee-Ya-Na, Yee-Ya-Na. Oh-le-de-aw Oh-he-Yong-de-aw. Ya-ha-Shing, Ya-ha-Tiem. Ai-Ying, Oh-le, Aw, Hee-Yahm . . . "

---

[1] Located near the northwest shore of the Dead Sea, site of an Essene community (about 100 BCE–68 CE), near a series of caves in which the Dead Sea Scrolls were found.

[2] Yee-Ya-Na means "I am."

3

Revealing My Secrets

To everything there is a season, and a time to every purpose under heaven.

—Ecclesiastes 3:1

IN THE MIDDLE of the night, about half a year after the onset of my automatic writing, I was preparing for an upcoming birthday party and everyone else in my house was asleep. An aroma began to envelop my body. It is hard to describe exactly what the scent was like, but the closest I can describe it is similar to myrrh. It was a pleasant aroma, and very alluring. I stopped fussing about the party and sat down on my couch because I understood that my attention was needed.

I immediately noticed that I was not alone in the living room; there were two special guests present. Sitting in one armchair opposite me was a spirit entity manifested as a gentleman dressed in a loose-fitting white ruffled blouse and dark trousers. He had dark hair and piercing blue eyes. In the other chair was a strikingly beautiful lady with long red hair and dark eyes. She wore a gown from the Victorian era. Rooted on my sofa, I watched as the two of them nodded, as if assessing and approving of me. Then they gave me the biggest smiles and vanished into thin air. This lady and the gentleman came to me many nights for more than a year in various costumes from the Victorian era. I always knew they were coming because before their arrival, my room would fill with the aroma of myrrh. I was also learning to see and hear thoughts from these two visitors. This always took place by way of telepathy; we never actually uttered a word.

During this early phase of my learning, I would try hard to hear with my ears. It seemed the spirits had other ideas, though, because as hard as I tried, I was not able to hear. Once I stopped trying, I could hear their thoughts in my head, and the information flowed more easily. I never heard the voices of the spirits with my ears, but the accent attached to this couple was very clear: it was definitely British.

I assume when my teacher felt I had sufficiently accomplished this lesson, it was time for the manifestations to leave and to test my ability without the benefit of sight. Thus my two friends never again showed themselves in ghostly forms. But I still smelled the aroma of myrrh and picked up the thoughts of my unseen friends. This was my only way of knowing it was them. Sometimes I was able to detect if one came without the other.

I truly believe my teacher planned the direction this form of learning took. I was treated like a child starting in kindergarten, and when I learned my lessons well, I graduated to the next step. I had to sneak hours from sleep time each night to do this. Finding the right time of day to learn from my teacher was hard, but with discipline and determination, I managed it.

In conjunction with the visitations by my ghostly friends, I was treated to sounds made by unseen hands and aromas that could not be accounted for. For example, I heard water coming from a closed faucet, smelled the delicious aroma of popcorn when none was popping, heard keys turning in locks and marbles rolling on a floor, and picked up the smell of freshly baked vanilla cookies, the sweet smell of pipe tobacco, and the many different scents of flowers, especially roses.

It was a joy to learn, and I never felt frightened. Perhaps the events of my childhood allowed for what I felt was a very natural progression. Although it may appear out of that range for most people, it did not seem so to me. I was an eager student willing to learn and grow and share it all.

During the 1970s I started to do some volunteer work at the local schools, and as a result, I began to meet more people of various backgrounds. One of them was a psychologist named Selina. Another was a psychiatrist named Ingrid, who was much older than Selina and I. The three of us became good friends.

One day while we were chatting, the topic suddenly shifted to dreams and being intuitive. By that time I had been longing to meet someone with whom I could discuss this topic, including the subject of *speaking to the dead.* I was less curious about other people's psychic abilities because I felt everybody possessed them. So I chanced telling them about myself. It was not an easy thing to do, but as luck would have it, they accepted me with open arms and told me, "The more you tried to hide this, the harder it was to keep the secret from surfacing."

They consoled me, adding, "Do not allow yourself to get sick of this. Allow us to help you ease your heart and your mind. Also allow us to help you understand you're not abnormal. Rather, you are an extension of being very normal. Perhaps you are supposed to do this."

They invited me to do some experiments. I was relieved to discover that they did not consider me a freak. Eager to find out all I could about what was happening, I sneaked away in the afternoons to meet with them at least a few times a week to explore my mediumistic and psychic ability.

During these experiments Selina would say, "Marilyn, tell me something about my past." I was able to tell Selina some of her personal history.

Selina confirmed that what I told her about her past had indeed happened. Then she said, "Marilyn, can you see anything in the future?"

I said, "Sure, you're going to have a baby boy."

She laughed aloud and said, "Oh, no, I cannot become pregnant. It's finished."

I reaffirmed, "Yes, you're going to have a baby boy. I don't know the exact timing or the circumstances surrounding your pregnancy, but you're going to have a little son."

Selina did want to have another child, but she did not believe it was possible. Nevertheless, one and a half years later, Selina gave birth to a healthy, full-term baby. The doctors were all amazed because they believed she would never have another child.

My friends were happy to work with me. I was finally accepted. My secret was out, and the best part was that I was not considered a freak.

During the time we were experimenting, Selina and Ingrid developed little tests for me. I also did Zener cards, which were very popular at that time. Originally developed by Karl Zener and Joseph Banks Rhine at Duke University, a deck of Zener cards consists of twenty-five cards printed with five simple symbols: a star, a circle, a square, a cross, and wavy lines. Five cards of each symbol are included in a deck, and the cards are viewed by one person, who tries to transmit the symbol via telepathy to another person (the receiver). My friend shuffled the cards by hand, and then selected one. I then tried to tell her which card she was sending. Sometimes she would ask me to tell her the order of a series of cards.

Some people score high on tests using these cards, but I failed miserably. To me, a card is a dead thing. If you were to draw a symbol on a piece of paper, blindfold me, and have me touch it, I would not do well at telling you what symbol you had drawn, but I could tell you a great deal about your life.

Ingrid found that I would be in the negative range of *psi*, which means psychic ability or psychic functioning. I consistently scored below average whenever I did a card test. The cards gave off such a cold sense that I truly felt blocked by them. But I was told that the reason I was so far in the negative curve was that I was so psychic!

Selina and Ingrid then asked me to enter a trance state, and they spoke with the entity James. Then I was given the Rorschach test, which required me to interpret inkblots, and an IQ test. They gave me standardized tests to make sure that I was healthy and I did not have a split personality or other delusions.

We also did psychometric experiments in which I held objects belonging to my friends or items collected from people I had never met. I usually scored well on this, too, because it involved getting a feeling for a person's life by touching an item that person owned. Then Ingrid and Selina would hide things and ask me to locate them. I did a very good job at finding the hidden items. For a while, I felt that I was like a lost-and-found bureau. This ability to find things seems to come and go. To this day, at times I am very good at it and other times I see nothing.

One day while we were talking, I said to Ingrid, "We have Little Piggy here for you."

Ingrid looked at me. Her mouth opened wide. She grabbed me so tightly I was almost smothered. I was worried and thought, "Oh, dear God, what did I do? Did I do something wrong?"

After Ingrid calmed down, she told me that she had lost a younger brother right after World War II, when she was very young. No one had spoken about him for many, many years. She immediately knew it was him. I asked her how she knew it was him and she said he was always called Little Piggy. She asked me how he was. At that time I was still developing my capability, and I honestly told her, "Truly, I don't know how he is." Still, Ingrid shed happy tears after she learned that her brother's spirit existed. She said, "You are a normal lady with extraordinary things happening."

Ingrid and Selina reassured me that I was not abnormal, that many others have a similar gift and the fact that mine started in my youth made it all the more important that I explore and expand this ability as much as possible. For years I had been nagging myself, "Am I inventing this? Am I doing something to cause this? And why am I different?" The weight of hiding my secret for so many years was finally lifted off my shoulders. I finally had friends to share my work with and to validate my normalcy. Our gatherings continued for many years until they both moved out of state.

4

The Spirit of
Eileen J. Garrett

*The gift of vision belongs to all. It links man to the
world he lives in, and by virtue of its magic not only
permits him to uncover the secrets of nature herself,
but may someday enable him to wrest the deep meaning of creation from the Universe.*

—Eileen Jeanette Garrett (1893–1970)

THE WISE LADY my control entity had mentioned years before
first communicated with me in the late 1970s. At that time I
was not aware of her true identity. When I asked her for her
name, she said, "Please call me Jenny." Yet during my early
days of automatic writing, she signed her name as "Eileen" for
about six years.

Portraits

In September 1978, during an early morning automatic writing
session, I drew the picture of a man's head. The man had a

39

slender face, long eyes, and heavy mustache (see Figure 4.1).
I am right-handed, but this picture was drawn with my left
hand. Under the picture was written boldly: "VOR at 25."

Around the picture were other words recording the questions I asked and the answers from the spirit. In this case, I
was particularly interested in finding the identity of this man.
The following is the dialogue recorded beside the face; the letters Q (for question) and A (for answer) are added for clarity.

> Q: Who is VOR?
>
> A: Ed.
>
> Q: Who's Ed?
>
> A: For Ellen.
>
> Q: Who's Ellen?
>
> A: Eileen
>
> Q: Still lives?
>
> A: He is your E.

Below "VOR at 25," more words were written.

> Q: Is this Vor?
>
> A: Yes.
>
> Q: Is this similar or more exact.
>
> A: Exact. He is blouse of light.
>
> Q: Ellen is Eileen?
>
> A: Yes.
>
> Q: Ed was me?
>
> Q: No.

I made another drawing in the same year showing a similar
face with bushy eyebrows. This face is wider than the first one,

Figure 4.1: First portrait of Ed.

but they share similar facial characteristics on noses, chins, mustaches, and eyes (see Figure 4.2). A short dialogue was also written on that picture.

Q: Who is this?

A: Ed.

Q: Who is Ed?

A: In your E—E & E is for you!

Q: What does this mean?

A: Eileen is you.

Q: Who is Ellen or Eileen?

A: Eileen Jen or Jeanette.

That is when I realized that Eileen was Jenny, the spirit entity I was communicating with, and that she probably had a past life as a man called Ellen. But who was Eileen or Eileen Jeanette? When I further questioned her about her identity, she wrote, "The matter of my full name is of no consequence to you." I wrote back "Ouch!" and that ended my inquiries about her identity for a very long time.

In the late 1980s, before the door to automatic writing was closed to me, a new door of communication opened. Eileen and James started to use my voice to communicate directly with other people. At that time I was a yoga teacher. Sometimes I would go into an altered state of mind in my class, and James and Eileen would come through me and talk using my voice. I had to rely on my students to tell me what had happened to me, since I was essentially unaware of the process.

Occasionally, after I came back to the conscious state, I was aware of which spirit had come through me to talk. Sometimes, I could remember fragments of the conversation. How-

Figure 4.2: Second portrait of Ed.

ever, they were just like scenes in dreams and they faded away quickly.

I found it inappropriate to fall into a full trance during a yoga class, so I stopped teaching yoga. Instead, I started to teach a new class—psychic development. This time I was not the only teacher, though. Eileen and James were with me.

One day in the early 1990s in my advanced psychic development class, I went into a full trance to let Eileen talk through me. Eileen revealed to my students that her full name is Eileen Jeanette Garrett.

So who was Eileen Garrett as a mortal? My students were as curious as I was about her. It turned out that Eileen Garrett was one of the most respected psychic mediums of the twentieth century. She had made tremendous contributions to the field of parapsychology.

Eileen Garrett was born in 1893 in Beauparc, County Meath, Ireland. Both of her parents committed suicide shortly after her birth. Eileen was raised by her aunt Martha.

Eileen was not alone during her childhood. She had three secret companions, two girls and a boy, whom she called "The Children." In her book *Many Voices*, she wrote, "They sought me. I did not have to go to them in any particular place or make any adjustments within myself in order to see them, be with them, or communicate with them freely" (Garrett 1968).

When Eileen told her aunt about The Children, her aunt ridiculed the idea and asked her to touch The Children. Eileen followed the suggestion. She later remembered the experience: "Their bodies were soft and warm. They were different. I saw all bodies surrounded by a nimbus of light, but 'The Children' were gauze-like. Light permeated their substance."

Eileen was a also a trance medium. When she was entranced, entities communicated through her. Her control was

Uvani, who claimed to have been a fourteenth-century Arab soldier. Abdul Latif, who claimed to have been a seventeenth-century Persian physician, was her contact for healing. When Eileen was mortal, she was not certain whether these entities were external or were simply part of her higher self. Therefore, she actively participated in scientific experiments.

Eileen received the attention of the whole world in the so-called R-101 Séances. On October 5, 1930, the 777-foot British dirigible R-101 crashed in flames near the French town of Beauvals, killing forty-eight of its fifty-four passengers. Two days after the crash, H. C. Irwin, captain of the R-101, un-expectedly came through Eileen Garrett while she was trying to communicate with Sir Arthur Conan Doyle, the creator of the fictional master detective Sherlock Holmes and the author of *The Lost World*, who had died on July 7 of that year. The séance had been requested by Harry Price, the director of the National Laboratory of Psychic Research, for Australian news-paperman Ian Coster.

During the séance, Irwin came through with a hesitant, anxious voice. He said, "The whole bulk of the dirigible was entirely and absolutely too much for her engine capacity. En-gines too heavy. It was this that made me on five occasions have to scuttle back to safety.... Useful lift too small. Gross lift computed badly ... Elevator jammed. Oil pike plugged.... Explosion caused by friction in electric storm. Flying to low altitude and could never rise. Disposable lift could not be uti-lized.... Fabric all water-logged and ship's nose is down. Im-possible to rise. Cannot trim ... Almost scrapped the roofs at Achy...." The whole communication was noted verbatim by Ethel Beenham, Price's secretary (Fuller 1978; Garrett 1968).

The transcript was analyzed by Will Charlton, the supply of-ficer of the R-101. After studying the report, Charlton and his colleagues described it as "an astounding document," containing more than forty highly technical and confidential details regarding the airship's fatal flight. It has so much confidential information that some people in England suggested arresting Eileen Garrett on suspicion of espionage.

Later on, Eileen came to the United States and wore different hats as a teacher, a lecturer, an author, and a publisher, who founded both *Tomorrow* magazine and Creative Age Press. Her most distinguished accomplishment was the founding of the Parapsychology Foundation in 1951.

In 1970, on attending the foundation's Nineteenth International Conference in the south of France, Eileen crossed over at the age of seventy-seven. When the spirit of Eileen Garrett recalled her own crossing-over experience, she said, "I did not attend my funeral. I was busy trying to figure out, was I really dead or was I 'here.' It was very confusing to me because it was like I was in a comatose state. I just kind of slipped in and out and I couldn't shake my own body up."[1]

Eileen and Me

Eileen's presence comes with a scent of strong perfumes, toilet water, and sometimes powder. When she is present, I sense the vibrant scents of iris, jasmine, Chanel No. 5, and a host of different flowers, all of which usually tend to gag me since I am allergic to perfume aromas.

She is witty and humorous. Sometimes she starts a conversation by saying, "Hello, I am initiating a celestial call. Please pick up."

Even though she does not manifest a physical body, I can sense her presence, her characteristics, and also the different

---

[1] Eileen is quoted here from a transcript of a trance session with Marilyn on June 2, 1996.

stages of her mortal life. Sometimes I see her as wild. I can feel her eyes twinkling as if her eyes are on mine, twinkling through me and allowing me to see things from her perspective. Many times I also see her in my mind's eye as a child of about six or seven years old, or when she was sixteen or seventeen and setting up house as a wife. I can also sense her as a young woman and as she is aging. All of a sudden she changes to her forties, with a full figure. I became so familiar with so many aspects of her that when her picture was shown to me years later, it did not surprise me at all.

Eileen developed lung illness when she was mortal. Sometimes when envisioning her I can pick up on her lung illness, magnifying my own. For this reason, I do not want to feel through certain stages of her life, because its feeds into my own health issues and tends to literally take away my breath.

Her personality is strong, sometimes gregarious, but always as a lady. Her manners are perfect. She is eloquent in her delivery and has a command over words. She often chides audiences during a séance, asking if she zipped over everyone's head.

When Eileen speaks, I am told there is a heightened energy in the room. Charismatic and enchanting, she is also clear in what she says. She oozes a magic that coaxes us to bring out the best in ourselves, to stop dawdling and actively pursue our dreams and goals, to the extent that they are real possibilities in life, and that more of our dreams are possible to attain than we might believe. She has a special charm that inspires those who hear her. Many people who have heard my beloved lady, who purports to be the spirit of Eileen Garrett, tell me that she is extremely witty, playing on words in a way that is sometimes confounding.

Eileen has told me that when she was mortal, she was a

tough businesswoman who refused to take no for an answer. When she wanted something, she would rush to get it done— which meant hard work for both herself and her employees. She reminisces about her work, and about those she worked with. Being lazy is a no-no to Eileen, and she will not tolerate it in me or in anyone else. She feels strongly that "words have power" and regards all writing as a gift to that end. When she is not satisfied with something I have said or done, she lets me know, as she did when she took me shopping for clothes years ago.

ᵃ ᵃ ᵃ

I usually dressed in casual New York City outfits unless she asked me to wear appropriate attire for a lecture. Eileen disregarded the fact that it was OK to wear jeans, slacks, boots, and plaid shirts. I loved that look, but she said I looked like a "hippie." Eileen told me she dressed quite differently in her lifetime. She dressed nicely, as if every day was an important occasion for her to celebrate. She told me that she had expensive taste because "it costs money to dress properly and look good." She had big issues with what I wore and how I looked.

Eileen asked if we might look in Saks Fifth Avenue and Lord and Taylor so that I would better understand her refined tastes and the type of clothing she wanted me to wear. Of course I could not turn her down, so we went—but I made a promise to her and to myself that it would only be to *look*, not to *buy*.

The day we spent looking was a worthy treat, and indeed I realized this lovely spirit lady had magnificent taste. It was an honor to hear her tell me how lovely I would look if I allowed her to dress me properly. Unfortunately, the price tags on the lowest-priced items were so far out of my reach that it was very clear we could only afford to look. She understood this, but it still did not stop her from taking me shopping in the hope that

I would weaken and buy something nice for myself.

Another day she asked if we could go clothes shopping at a local boutique. Eager to please and still feeling slightly in awe of her, I said yes. Thus began some of the funniest events to take place between mortal and spirit.

The day started out pretty much as usual. We walked many miles over the Brooklyn Bridge, down to Chinatown, over to the East Village, then to the West Village, circling back to the World Trade Center, and back over the Brooklyn Bridge. Somewhere in the middle of this seven-mile journey, I found myself in an expensive boutique. I had no memory of entering the place. It was as if Eileen had taken control of my feet and guided me into the store. I was completely unaware of what transpired until my arm, which was weighed down with dresses, suits, slacks, blouses, belts, and even two bags, became so heavy that I was brought back to a fully conscious state. Upon awakening I was embarrassed to find my items were being placed down on the counter in front of the cash register, ready to be checked out. There was a gentle tug of war going on between Eileen and me. It was as if my left hand kept holding on to the clothing, while my right hand was pulling them away to give back to the clerk. And I kept sensing Eileen yelling into my head to *please* buy these clothes. As the clerk began to ring up my items, I feigned illness and escaped without too much fuss.

I walked out of the store with a very red face, and I yelled in my head at Eileen: "Dammit! Dammit! Dammit! How could you do this to me? I'm so embarrassed! Oh, my God. I should never walk back into that store again."

I felt my whole body rumble with laughter. Then a crystal-clear message came through. "Go back in. Do not run away. Just pick up a beautiful scarf and maybe one or two little items."

I was halfway down the block. I turned around and I went back into the store. I did exactly as I had been told.

Eileen apologized to me and said, "I realize you don't have money in your pocket to be so extravagant, but you look so pathetic. I cannot stomach you in dungarees and in a pea jacket and a hat over your head. You look like a bag lady."

I said, "But it keeps me warm."

Later Eileen taught me how to shop. In the past I had no idea there was a secret underground where one could shop for inexpensive but really fine clothing. The clothes are barely worn and kept in consignment shops.

James had his own ideas about what I should wear. He wanted me to wear long skirts that went all the way to my ankles and blouses that covered my neck, arms, and wrists. Each of my spirit friends wanted me to dress differently, in accordance with what they deemed to be proper. One day I said, "I'm always clean and shower daily. When I represent you in lectures, classes, séances, TV, or radio work, I will try my best to wear appropriate attire. Do not worry."

Eileen is still not deterred from wanting to teach me how to dress, and she still gives her opinion when I go shopping. She says, "Marilyn, this is beautiful," and she puts my hand on something gorgeous that I cannot afford to buy.

In addition to our dressing styles, there are other differences between us. She likes perfume. I cannot tolerate perfume—it causes my asthma to flame up. She loves jewelry, but I cannot wait to take it off. She is outspoken and gregarious; I am quiet and conservative. She is controlling; I am not.

Eileen is a spirit full of passion. She sometimes tells me, "Oh, stop being so dowdy." Or she will say, "Snap out of it, Marilyn." She once told me that she would be like *Hello, Dolly!*

if we compared her with a passionate female from the theater.

Colors have a special meaning to her and she remembers them as being very alive, with feelings embracing her existence. She once said to my students, "If I saw yellow I would feel the liver and kidney areas, which, of course, does not always follow what the average person might find. Color radiates in different places for me and of course they can disappear. Sometimes colors can show where a sickness is."

One time she treated me to just a tiny little bit of what she experienced and felt in her life when she was a mortal and from the point of view of a spirit. She took me on a journey through purple.

She had me focus on a little bronze statue, and she asked, "Now, what do you see?"

I said, "I see purple."

Eileen said, "Look again."

I was standing approximately twelve feet away from the object as the color purple took life. It was swirling round and round until it grew very big. With each display of its radiant color it showed itself from its palest shade to its deepest hue. Then it reached across the room to where I was standing. It adhered itself to my body by first cocooning me in its color and then by entering every pore of my skin. I remember the sensation of tingling and a calmness coming over me. The experience was awesome. Then I heard the voice of purple in my head, and it was a female humming while playing a harp.

Eileen asked, "What do you feel?"

I was speechless.

"Marilyn," she said, "that's just a little of what I used to take in almost daily."

I finally said to her, "You were and still are an incredible person."

And she laughed and said, "Of course."

The Spirit World

Called "the Courier of Light" by James, Eileen connects people to the spirit realm.

What follows is a compilation of excerpts taken over five years of taped sessions during different trance states when Eileen spoke through me. These quotes are taken directly from the tape recordings, and even though the language is somewhat awkward and unusual in places, we did not alter it.

Eileen says that mind (which can also be called soul, spirit, ghost, or entity) is "energy that has intelligence and emotion." Minds are all connected, and together they form the "collective consciousness," which can be further grouped into the following categories: the connected collective consciousness of man, the connected collective unconsciousness of man, the collective consciousness of the universe, and the collective consciousness of spirit. Every mind contributes to the collective consciousness and is affected by the collective consciousness.

She loves to say, "To think of thinking is to think a thought, which must connect to our thinking." She also says, "We always visualize our thoughts." Thinking is the creative force of the world, and thoughts affect all forms of lives. The spirit world is filled with lives.

Eileen speaks often about thoughts and atoms and the interconnection between them. She says, "If atoms are ruling me, then they have a regard for thinking." In other words, consciousness exists even in atoms. Eileen gives a helpful suggestion that "for those doing serious work on the survival theory, the focus should be placed on atoms."

In the spirit world, she says, "there is no past, present, and future so the word 'time' is not a normal feeling for us."

Conceptually, everyone has a tower that contains the file of our lives and the history of who we are.

She also says, "We deal in yin and yang philosophy, which is female and masculine, yin being female and yang being masculine. Understand that we can project our thoughts and create whatever we want, so that if there are men and women here, of course their essences are remaining with their consciousness as they present it. But there is a very neutralizing feeling. So it is mostly just an energy that can think."

Regarding sex in the spirit world, she says, "It cannot take place without bodies. But you can have mental sex if you take it to that extreme. But truly it is boring."

The mind can be fragmented, too. The mind can exist in several places at the same time. One day Eileen asked me if I sensed anything different about her. I did not detect anything. She was happy to hear my answer, because she was fragmenting her thoughts while being elsewhere to attend to a friend's funeral. What she was able to offer me was still intact even though her thoughts were simultaneously elsewhere. She chuckled and said, "It is wonderful getting used to not dealing in your space-time continuum."

When Eileen was mortal, she did not believe in reincarnation. She was not even sure whether Uvani and Abdul Latif were really spirit entities or simply some aspects of herself. Now, as a spirit, she says, "I didn't believe in reincarnation, but look at me now!" She adds, "My thoughts on reincarnation have greatly expanded into believing that there is an existence of a continuation." In one séance, she spoke of the change in her beliefs with regard to the writings she made when she was mortal: "I am going to rewrite what I wrote. It will be the proof that the mind exists, but not as you know it with the space-time continuum."

Eileen gives a very detailed description regarding what happens when we cross over. She says, "When you leave your body, and many of you leave it before the actual death, what actually leaves the body is the spirit, the part of you that is intelligent, not the brain, but the memory in the brain. Did you hear me? It is the memory in the brain which is a substance, a light force. It has the memory of each lifetime in it. We have termed it 'spirit' or 'entity.' It usually comes out of the top of your head and filters up toward wherever you are. It hovers above you a bit, sometimes for about two days, until it dissipates slowly. Sometimes it will fly around in the company of the body. That is who you are. You then have the memory of that existence you just came from. Because it was, for instance, a long day, you have a lot of memory. You have time to recall, time to go through it and review and to meet and greet those you knew."

"When it is a traumatic death—like sudden death or a murder, since there are no accidents—what occurs is that your essence that just left you and guided you is almost in shock, amazed that it is no longer in the body, so the death experience is total. The body now is resting below and you are looking down upon yourself, poking it, and even saying, 'I can't do anything.' Because it was a bit traumatic, you kind of stay with it for a while. You want to find out what went wrong. Is it a dream? For those people, it can take upward of ten to twenty or thirty years before they will leave that which they had in that lifetime, either good or bad."

"When you are *home*, if you want to contact other entities here, you think the thought and they will appear," Eileen says. "It is not easy for everyone here to think instantly. You are a thought, but usually a thought of the occurrence of what brought you here. Then you view your lifetime as though on a

TV screen and you say, 'Wow, I did a wonderful job in that life. I played my role so well. I was supposed to be the beggar or the farmer or the mayor or the priest or what have you. And look at that. I did it all and I did it the way I was supposed to do it.'"

Eileen reveals a reincarnation theory different from that generally held in Eastern philosophy. She says, "The life you lead, in a sense—and as I tell you this, don't get upset—is the only life you will ever have as to who you are now. But when you come home you continue to live. You do come back to have another existence. It is never, never as the person you were. Nor do you reincarnate to a lesser person than you were. You always go higher. So imagine, when you sit in judgment of the criminal who murdered someone, don't be too sure that that criminal deserved such severe judgment. In a way, in an obscure way, that criminal took on the burden of your society to do those nasty things, to raise your thoughts, so that your consciousness becomes more compassionate and caring. Many of you are still Neanderthal or maybe Cro-Magnon."

In many of our séances, Eileen has told those who ask about angels that their perception is far from what the heavenly thought is. She makes it perfectly clear that there are no winged entities flying about in heaven, and that angels with wings are a figment of one's imagination. But she adds that since thought is collected in man's conscious mind as well as in his unconscious mind, as often as not one quickly realizes that the manifestation created from the thought about angels is an illusion and has always been one. When they arrive in the afterlife and look for those winged angels, they are met with intelligent, loving beings whose job is to teach people what angelic love is.

Furthermore, Eileen tells us that there are no master entities in the spirit world that are higher than the others. She says, "That is a silly notion. There are people making a lot of money from this idea. I tell you and caution you that if you limit yourself and believe that you are not as high as a so-called master, then you will never get there."

According to Eileen, there are map-outs in our lives and there are free choices as well, "in a very odd way." She says, "I can tell you that we choose what we do in our living. We do have free choice. We do choose our desires. We never do choose our destiny, even if you think you do. It is pre-ordained."

When you are a spirit, you choose your own map-outs based on the need of your soul. "You do through your soul," Eileen explains with examples: "Now, if the soul indeed hasn't learned what it is to be cruel and mean, it might enjoy learning if only from an aspect of being abused. That is the abused syndrome. Now, if the soul has no idea what it means to be aggressive and nasty and cruel, it might learn what it is to be the abuser. Think about the abuser and the abused. How perfect it is in predesigning their marriage, or between children and family members or friends. They accommodate both of the souls' needs in that one lifetime, but they do not have to stay together eternally. So the soul grew even though one in your society is called the meanie and the other the wimp. Now, people develop guilt and when you come home, and I love calling where we are in paradise home, we accept you as you are. It matters little to us if you were killing people. What does matter is that those around you receive enough information of what they deem to be tasteless, and grow from that."

There are rarely accidents in our lives—they are mostly pre-ordained. We set up our own destinies, all kinds of destinies, which can be as strange as being murdered in a lifetime. Asked

whether a person could forgive his own murderer in the afterlife, Eileen said, "Absolutely! Not only did he do that, shocking
as that is to believe, and I know you don't accept it, but that's
all right because you are more evolved in your way of thought,
but he also forgave his murderer. There are very few in your
world who can forgive their enemies. The thought about people
evolving is correct. You do evolve with each existence. Even
if the last existence was superb, you may go back and have
a very lousy one. It is the need of the soul's journey that
it must experience lousy, because it didn't before. It doesn't
know comparison. It doesn't know the real definition of love."

Eileen says that all souls are already in perfection. Every
soul in existence is in perfection. Those who communicate
with us are using the imperfect thought pattern program of
the existing mortal. "You understand that it keeps us limited
at best," she says. "We are not coming to you in any other form
but perfection. When you come home, you can only be perfection. That is why, when you read your Bible that examines evil
and evil spirits, and evil this and evil that, we here giggle. Now
I am not saying that poltergeist activity doesn't exist, but what
I am saying is that they cannot be evil. That is your man-made
conception, induced in you through your religion. When you
meet us, we can only be perfect. We may not be conducive in
the feelings that you might desire, but we are in perfection. In
that perfect state we come to you from different areas of the
heavens."

She explains, "Your mortal existence is for growth and the
sojourn of the soul is to exclaim itself. The excitement of each
living is an exemplification of trying out the existence of that
humanness. It is involved with the many growing things you
have to grow from. If somebody is old and handy at dispensing
potions, let's say, before medicine became a thing of esteemed

knowledge, if somebody was involved in herbs and was offering healings, that person was regarded with shamanistic abilities of being among the highest and holiest. That is man-made nonsense. He or she is not among the highest. You deem it so because you judge what is human acceptance for the society that you lived in at the time."

"You decide when your spirit goes into another life. The soul is the big boss. The soul is intellectual energy. It decides, it deems, it creates. You are given the capacity of the power of that soul." Then she talked about the soul nucleus, the master soul: "For instance, in the soul nucleus of mine, Marilyn existed in several lifetimes with me and she spoke through me as someone else for a different lesson, for sure. You have to realize that 'here' is your nucleus. From the nucleus are many different existences. Each one of those existences is for the spirit's sojourn in a living. That is why you can have a simultaneous existence and feel like you are a twin to somebody over in Egypt. Did I lose you? Here is the nucleus. We call this boss. The boss is your soul, that one soul. Imagine spokes on a wheel. Do you have that vision? Each spoke is a different existence, not necessarily at a different time. Each existence is a part for the growing of its incarnated life, its sojourn for that soul to feel what it was like."

She says that the spoke, the life experience, does start with number one and it does go around and around and the spiral gets wider and wider: "We then have completed everything there is to complete. Unless, of course, if we begin to manifest a new concept of life, the spiral begins again. Then we have to exemplify all the things that are to that new form of life. By the way, ladies and gentlemen, you will experience a new form of life."

"A fragment of a soul can exist. An aspect of a soul can exist. But there is also something called *the fusion of many minds.*" Eileen says, "Ten human beings can be fused and merged into one consciousness. That one consciousness can have ten different lives at the same time in ten different places plus the past, present, and future of all of them going on simultaneously. So the fusion of the thinking of all that is amazing, isn't it?"

Eileen says that human spirits can only come back as humans. "You cannot come back as a tree if you are human. You can experience in the interim to feel like that tree. You place that thought through what you now call consciousness, which is all of the same to us here. You place that thought of the tree, and experience it, but you do not become the tree. You do not sprout branches." Nor can we come back as animals. They have souls and self-consciousness just like us. However, "the animal world does evolve on its own through natural evolution. Man chooses to only be man. The animal kingdom only chooses their way. But it is not a consciousness like what humans are engulfed with."

Eileen frequently talks about ecology and how we must all pitch in to help save our planet from further decay. She explains, "Earth will have many changes. If man is growing, does the earth grow with him? Of course. You evolve, not alone, but Earth evolves along with you. You must all adapt to each other. Your planet is very much alive. So your planet will be of such a nature to accommodate who you are because you will need sustenance. But perhaps the sustenance will not be that which you have now. You won't be able to cut a cow open and eat it. But you will have something that will be just as satisfactory. I am giving you a glimpse of where you are going. Create your thinking to collect your thoughts and you have perfection. You cannot adjust your life to live in that perfection because everyone around you isn't there yet."

She also says, "I am concerned about ecology and pollution of the air not because I worried as a mortal, but because I have certain insights. As all of you know, I had a passion for this beautiful Earth and I worried often and I still am worrying about the death of the planet. You are ruining your earth. You are polluting it with everything that you do. You have created a terrible atmosphere. Most of you will have to wear masks in your futures. There will come a time when you will not be able to go outdoors because the pollution will be so bad."

The greatest source of life energy is love. Eileen says, "Love is prevalent in everything we do and when I use that word 'love,' it is to be taken with deep consideration that love is the highest source of energy for us all. It is more than an emotion and becomes a very alive thing." A mortal experience is "a celebration of life" and when it nears its end it becomes "a completion of love."

5

Chinese Medicine Woman

Do not be desirous of having things done quickly. Do not look at small advantages. Desire to have things done quickly prevents their being done thoroughly. Looking at small advantages prevents great affairs from being accomplished.

—Confucius (551–479 BCE)

THERE IS ANOTHER female entity named June who has been with me for almost as long as James has. She does not talk much, but I sense that she has something to do with the mechanics of how this mediumship ability works.

If other spirits feel like plush, soft cotton, the sense I get for June is akin to down feathers swaying in a gentle breeze.

She is short. When she comes close to me, I can feel her height is about five feet one inch, or perhaps less. I sense she has a pointy nose; high, full cheekbones; thin lips; and long grayish hair tightened up into a bun away from her face. She is about in her fifties or sixties, but her spirit is young. She wears no glasses, but she squints her eyes so it looks like she

should be wearing glasses. She does not have any jewelry on
at all. She wears a baggy outfit consisting of a dark top over
dark trousers. She never wears anything on her feet. Her feet
tend to turn outward when she walks.

The first time I was introduced to her, I asked teasingly,
"June, who are you?"

She said, "I am your wise one."

It might have been June who relayed the message for my
neighbor during an automatic writing session in the 1970s.
On the page was written "Hello, and I love you" in Chinese. It
appeared to be a message from the grandmother of my neighbor. I asked James if he wrote Chinese and he said, "No." So I
assume the message was given by June.

June is amazing. She says little, but whenever she needs
me to learn something or get a message to someone, her determination is strong. I am comforted by her presence. Her
wisdom always shines through.

June comes to me when she feels there is a need for me to
learn something. She favors communicating with me during
my dream states. During these times she will tell me to go to
the cliff. The cliff is a sacred learning place for me. When we
are there, she gently waves her arms toward a vast field that
is surrounded by sloping hills, with gigantic mountains as the
backdrop. Then, with hand gestures, she sends hundreds of
wild horses down from the mountains into the field. These
horses listen to her every command, never spoken by mouth
but given with gestures. The movement of her hands seems to
make harmonic sounds that stir these wild horses into action.
I watch in awe as they come thundering down past my sacred
cliff. One horse in particular always slows as it approaches
me. Its body is all white, with eyes that beckon to me to go
with it. As strange as it may sound, I believe this horse and I

know each other. I feel that this horse once belonged to me in a past life.

After the horses are settled in the field, June begins my lesson. Sometimes she has me study flowers that grow wild in the field. She shows me which are good for eating and which are good to use as healing remedies. The same goes for small trees. She is considerate of the beauty that nature gives when pointing to a flower or tree. She makes them come alive with sounds and thus I am able to hear the lovely music our plant world makes.

June gently guides me throughout all our journeys. I will walk anywhere with her. She shows me where to walk and what sounds to listen to. All these enlightening teachings are done slowly on my behalf, so I can appreciate the offerings from nature as well as take time to see the majestic beauty that is always present.

June has expressed to me that she has never believed that one can learn quickly. She feels that learning is a process that takes time. She stresses this point, adding that if I tried to do things quickly, she would walk away. She said my lessons had a lot to do with learning patience and understanding that it takes patience to learn, grow, and share.

June comes to me alone. She may very well be a fragment spirit of James, but her presence when visiting me is always alone. There are not hundreds of other people or entities associated with her. I always feel that it is June and James who do the healing. James empowers my body through some kind of energy, and June directs it.

June looks like a medicine woman, a person who collects herbs used to heal people. She walks into fields and knows which leaves, flowers, roots, stems, scrapings from the bark of trees, and a host of other items to collect. She has a little bag tied on her side into which she puts her collected items. I do not know what is in there. Her healing remedies come from a garden in heaven.

I suffer from weak lungs and have had several bouts with pneumonia, plus asthma and a light case of emphysema. June suggested I eat water chestnuts. She said if I ate a small portion of them a few times a week they would purify the lungs. She told me to wash them thoroughly and steam them for a few minutes. I cooked them and found they did indeed help alleviate the pressure in my lungs.

Many years later, I learned that water chestnut is used in Chinese herbal medicine as an expectorant.

Another time, she reminded me of my grandmother. She said, "You should use cornstarch."

"For what?" I asked her.

She said, "With feet. Put cornstarch in your shoes. You walk a lot."

I followed her advice and sprinkled cornstarch in my shoes. My feet kept cool and dry during my seven-mile-a-day walk.

June emphasized the importance of fasting once a week, telling me that fasting is the simplest and most efficient way of relieving the overloaded system. I have practiced this detoxification for more than forty years. I have found that I appreciate food more after I finish fasting.

June also told me how to get rid of little aches and pains. She was very happy when I learned about the meridian lines that run throughout the body. She is confident that people can alleviate pain by gently pressing the correct meridian lines rather than having needles placed into them. In other words, she favors acupressure over acupuncture.

June does not believe in strenuous exercises, but she firmly believes in walking and learning how to breathe properly.

When I taught yoga to senior citizens, June would correct the way I taught breathing. She would mentally say, "No, you're going too fast." I listened to her and slowed down my pace.

I never buy cookbooks, but with June's guidance I am full of creativity in cooking. When it comes to cooking, June sometimes guides my hands to use certain spices to flavor our food. I had always thrown away the stem of the broccoli before June taught me not to do so. Rather, she taught me how to peel and cut the broccoli to allow the sweet flavor to come out.

Many years ago I did not know how to pick a melon. June placed my thumb at the base of the melon so I could feel whether it was ripe. To make sure that her advice was correct, I verified with a produce man. He said, "Of course. Now you have to shake it like you are buying a watermelon. So listen to how it sounds."

Grocery shopping became an art. I looked up snow peas and she would pick up the best. June would not necessarily pick up those that looked the best. She always said, "Look between the packages and look up the stamps carefully. If it is hard and discolored, then it is no good."

With tomatoes, I was educated to let go of those that were mushy and soft. They have to be firm but have color. I often chose the ones that were too ripe. She would guide me to those that were not quite ripe yet.

One day I wanted to buy plum tomatoes, which are oblong instead of round. She would not let me buy any; she kept moving my hands over to the bigger, rounder tomatoes. I just let my hand glide with her guidance. It was rewarding because the tomatoes she chose were perfect. I used to live on a twentieth-floor apartment in New York City. Vegetables tended to spoil quickly, probably due to the changes of temperature, pressure, and moisture. June must have considered the atmosphere, or maybe she gave the vegetables a magic touch, because no vegetable I bought with her ever spoiled.

Sheree's Reflections on June

In July 2003 Victor and I met Marilyn Raphael in Las Vegas. When we were talking in a hotel room, all of a sudden Marilyn said several times, "I need more oxygen." Then she fell into a full trance. Then the spirits of Eileen and James came and talked to us using her voice.

Since it had been noted to us beforehand that there may be a previous connection or some unfinished business between Marilyn and me, Victor asked Eileen, "Have Marilyn and Sheree met before?"

"Yes, they were both in a sugar field in China in the 1500s," Eileen answered.

"Sugar field?" I said.

"Yes, sugar field. Not cotton field. Not rice field. Sugar field!"

I was puzzled, and I questioned this information and asked an aunt, Helen Hwang, a physician from China, a few days later, "Where do Chinese plant sugar, Aunt Helen?"

My aunt smiled amicably and said, "Well, definitely not in the central part of China. Southern China; namely, Fujian and Guangdong."

Then, in February 2004, while doing research for this book, I found an academic report that later gave Marilyn, Victor, and me chills.

According to Dr. Victoria Cass (Cass 1986), during the Chinese Ming dynasty in the 1500s, women doctors of medicine, herbalists, and shamans flourished in Fujian and Guangdong. Those female specialists contrast sharply with their male counterparts in terms of training. Instead of formal training with medical college and textbooks, the women doctors acquired their knowledge by common practice.

After we learned this, we could not help but think of June's knowledge of herbs and holistic treatment although she had no formal education, and Eileen's revelation about when and where Marilyn and I had met in a past life.

In August 2004 Eileen revealed that June had been associated with her in her own lifetime. Uvani brought June in, representing her to Eileen as a man called Abdul Latif. June came to her as the spirit form of that male healer. Apparently June belongs to the same clan—same soul. As a part of the soul clan, she had other lives as a healer, as a real doctor.

Eileen's disclosure surprised both Marilyn and me. Aren't our lifetimes like plays? We play different roles in different lifetimes. The discovery of the same soul revealing different spirit identities to different mortals is like watching actors acknowledging their curtain calls. We know that they are bowing to us in their off-play identity, but we are enjoying their bowing with their costumes on.

6

An Enriched Life

We fear things in proportion to our ignorance of them.
—Livy (59 BCE–17 CE)

THE ENDEARING SPIRITS enrich my life on a daily basis. I sense them with me while I am driving, eating, and occasionally drinking. I feel they have saved my life in certain cases and also stopped me on occasion from looking like the town fool or being very embarrassed in other cases. Below are some inter- actions that show why I feel this way.

Native American Boy

During the first several years of my work with spirits, I had many questions and struggles to overcome. I felt that if one day in the future my work and involvement should become public, I would first and foremost need some kind of proof to myself that they did indeed exist and were not a figment of my imagination. I also felt that if I was going to allow my body to be controlled by another form of existence, protecting it from harm's way would be of utmost importance. Therefore,

I decided to challenge their existence with my greatest fear—snakes.

On a hot summer day I went alone to the top of a mountain range that had a small plateau with red shale rock and hundreds of birch trees. I knew there were rattlesnakes in upstate New York. I did not know at the time that the birch forest on top of that mountain had been rumored to have been used as an old Native American burial ground. I remember thinking that it looked like any other upstate New York forest. The challenge was set and there was no turning back.

My feet were literally guided to the spot where I was to have this test. Thus my trust factor increased greatly, as did my faith, which I instinctively knew would be tested in a gentle way. I still had a great deal of fear of the yet-to-be, only slightly quelled by my gut sensing of the spirits based upon the fact that they had already guided me to the spot for the test. Snakes did and still do frighten me greatly. So with more of a determined approach and feeling a bit safer, I surrendered to what was to happen. I recall in my somewhat afraid and naive way saying to the spirits, "If you're really with me and you are not just in my imagination, please show me your protection. If I am to do this work, you must show me that you can protect me and help me challenge my fear of snakes." I was shocked at the fact that I even had enough courage to take on the challenge.

I closed my eyes. I heard the definite sound of rattlesnakes. I thought I saw something from the corner of my eye. I looked around and saw several snakes coming out from behind the rocks and below the bushes. They did not appear to be coming toward me, but, because of my phobia, I felt that every snake in the world was coming toward me. I was pouring sweat and felt very cold.

Standing all alone approximately thirty feet from me was the spirit of a young boy. From his appearance I assumed it was the spirit of a Native American boy. He must have been seven or eight years old. I stayed focused, looking at him, while the snakes came closer and closer. While this was happening, I had another sensing and I recall the lovely sound of a flute being played. I did not know instruments well, but I just knew the sound belonged to a flute. The tune was alluring and allowed me to concentrate my thoughts on surrendering to the spirits while disassociating myself from the big challenge of the test that I set up for myself.

I thought, "Oh, this is very funny. Now all I need to do is see someone with a basket and a snake charmer come out."

Although I was in a calmer state, it was not enough to quiet my nerves completely, and I recall feeling very queasy. I was about to faint because there were several snakes down by my feet. I started to sway and get nauseous. I was scared.

This little boy put his finger up to his mouth, signaling me to be quiet. I immediately balanced myself as gracefully as possible, with my feet twirled around each other and my arms twirled to reach up toward the sky. As a yoga teacher, I realized that I was inadvertently standing in *Vrksasana* (tree pose).

The next thing I knew, the little boy came toward me, and every single snake that was near me was following him. I assumed he came toward me to have those near my feet go with him, too. I was no longer as afraid and had a greater feeling of harmony and being at ease that was like a veil, enveloping my mind and body. I watched while this young boy took care in the gentlest of ways to get all those snakes to follow him. I still heard the flute playing in my head. It was not eerie. It actually had a very soothing effect.

My hands were unlocked from the tree pose and brought

back down to my side. My feet were apart. I was drenched in sweat. I looked around and the forest was empty. I was the only one there. Another sensation overtook me as I came to my full consciousness. Although I was greatly relieved that the test was over and my challenge was met, the ordeal left me exhausted and I desperately needed to sit down because my knees were wobbly. I thought I was up there for ten minutes. When I came down and looked at my clock, I saw that almost four hours had passed.

I then told James that I would do the work he asked me to do as a connector for the spirit realm and I had gained a great deal of inner peace and a healthy trust for the spirit, to whom I definitely would entrust my mortal life. I learned several lessons that day, among which is this: Watch out for what you ask for.

Lesson on a Bus

Lessons keep happening.

One day in the 1970s, while I was sitting in the back of a crowded Brooklyn bus, a very tall woman, perhaps six feet tall, with a gigantic amount of hair got on the bus. Her height, hairstyle, and high-heeled shoes made her almost touch the ceiling inside the bus.

This lady struggled to the rear of the bus and was headed directly toward where I was sitting. Panic set in because as she came closer to me, a very strong aroma of the perfume she was wearing was gagging me, and my very breath was being cut off.

I was having a severe allergic reaction to this lady's perfume and I needed her to go away from me as quickly as possible. Knowing the bus was very crowded and there was hardly room for anyone to move, I felt what was needed was some help from the spirit world or some powers from the universe or a cosmic force. I recall saying over and over again, "Please, someone help me because I will surely die if I continue to inhale these noxious fumes that are taking my breath away." I kept a strong vision of her moving toward the front of the bus. To my amazement, as I repeated this mantra, she started to move away from me, toward the front of the bus.

As this lady was responding to my silent pleas and moving away from me, I saw a shocking thing happen to her. A giant roach fell down from the ceiling right into her hair. I immediately said to myself, "Oh God, I didn't mean that. Oh God, please forgive me."

I could not believe what was happening to this lady and I became disgusted with the situation and needed to get off the bus as quickly as possible. I was afraid that the whole bus was full of cockroaches. The woman saw me get up and she rushed past me. I did not know whether I should tell her that a cockroach just dropped into her hair. I remember looking at her, and she started to shake her head. Then I said, "Oh, Madam, there is a bug in your hair. It came from the ceiling." The bus stopped and I got off. The woman screamed, and the whole bus filled with passengers went crazy. People were pushing and yelling at each other in their hurry to get off that bus.

I had willed the woman away from me, but I didn't wish her an incident like that. I was learning, developing my abilities, and I learned that willing for something to happen sometimes causes other events, creating a reaction that, in this case, set an otherwise quiet bus into total chaos. One must be very careful for what they wish for, or, in this case, what they *will* for.

The lesson here is to always use the willing exercise in

a positive way, especially toward those whom you may truly dislike or who cause you to become frustrated and annoyed. Never *will* a person sickness or other negative consequences. I truly believe that what you put out there in thought and action will eventually come back to you. Treat others with kindness and lots of love and watch how the universe rewards you with a bounty of the same.

Save Me

My old apartment in Brooklyn Heights, New York, is on the twentieth floor of a high-rise building. More than six hundred people live in this building and there are three elevators to service them. It is not uncommon for one or sometimes two of the elevators to be out of service. On rare occasions all three are out at the same time.

On one brutally cold, icy winter day, I was returning home from my usual daily walk. The cold weather mixed with the ice and rain caused me to need the use of a restroom immediately. I raced into my building and saw that all three elevators were broken; they only went up a few floors and then stopped. There were no restrooms on the ground floor, and the basement bathroom was broken. The hallway was getting crowded, and there were more than twenty people waiting for an elevator.

I thought, "Oh, I am not going to make it. I will wet myself in front of all my neighbors and die of embarrassment."

Then I thought, "Wait a minute. Calm down. Calm down."

Silently I spoke with my spirit control, James, and asked—or perhaps begged—him to please take away this urgency to urinate and save me from dying of embarrassment. I was breaking out in a sweat even though it was freezing in the lobby. I tried hard to be polite and make conversation with neighbors, all the while fighting off my urge and pleading with the spirit to help me.

Several intense minutes went by and then the urge passed! This was a miracle considering how awful my circumstances had been just a few minutes before. The desire faded and I was able to focus on the present issue of waiting for an elevator or walking up the twenty flights to my apartment.

Eventually an elevator door opened. Everybody piled into it. Accompanied with a strong gut feeling, I heard in my mind: "Don't take it. Hold back. Start walking the stairs."

I walked the stairs and made it to the thirteenth floor before the urge came back to me. I thought I would pass out before I could take another step, so I got out of the stairwell, feeling foolish but believing that help would come from the spirit. I waited for an elevator even though they were broken and getting one would take a miracle. Once again I found myself begging for help over a ridiculous situation.

I pushed the button and within a few seconds an elevator came. It was empty, which caused me a little concern, but I trusted the spirit as he told me, "You can get into this elevator." (Keep in mind that I never hear voices, so this communication comes to me through my mind and a very strong sense of what is being told to me.)

As the elevator door closed and I slowly went up seven floors, I kept saying "thank you" to my beloved James, who had once again come to my rescue. As I got off the elevator I felt the sensation of gliding to my front door. It felt as though my feet never touched the hallway floor, as if the spirit was carrying me into my apartment. Once I was inside, the urge returned and I was able to take care of the pressing matter.

Here is what I learned would have happened if I had not listened to James and took the elevator from the lobby: I would have found myself trapped with twenty other people in an over-crowded elevator that was stuck for more than an hour. Given my circumstances this would have been awful for me.

The elevator I used remained broken for two more days. Interestingly enough, several of my friends were confounded that it worked for me because there was a notice in the lobby asking people to please not use this elevator. Apparently the notice was up during the time the elevator worked for me.

James had once again saved me. Although it may not seem like an important thing in the grand scheme of things, had he not interceded I would have been mortified and embarrassed in front of my neighbors.

Greetings from the New York City Policeman

In the late 1970s Pope John Paul II was visiting New York City and would be passing my street corner. I was as excited as everyone else to catch a glimpse of this beloved man.

Early that morning before the policemen lined the streets to set up the barricades, I took my 165-pound English bull mastiff for his walk in the park across the street from my building. Leaving the park to return to my house I saw the police were very busy lining themselves up, as each officer had his assigned place to stand.

As I crossed the street, a policeman came over to me. He was about six feet six inches tall and his height alone was enough to frighten me. I thought I was going to get a ticket for jaywalking.

He said to me, "May I speak to you?"

I said, "Yeah, is it about my dog?"

He replied, "No. It's about that wonderful spirit that walks with you."

I felt honored and said, "Oh, thank you." Although I seldom

looked people in the face on the streets in New York, I looked at him.

He continued, "Can I hold your hand?"

I answered, "Of course."

"You know," he said, "you walk with one of the holiest spirits in the world."

I kept silent throughout this. He added through little sobs, "Maybe I am just caught up with the emotions of the day. I'm telling the truth, ain't I?"

I replied, "Yes, you are."

He asked my name and I told him. He then said, "Do you know my name? Because the spirit who's with you knows who's with me."

I reluctantly answered, looking him right in the eyes, "Your name is Moses."

He stepped two steps back and sighed. Then he took out his driver's license and asked me, "What's my first name?"

"Moses."

"Marilyn, please introduce me to the young spirit you walk with," he said.

I told him who it was. The policeman named Moses was as touched and as overwhelmed as I was. It was a mutual experience filled with an understanding of sensing, seeing, and joining as one in the belief of the existence of spirits.

Episodes like this occur from time to time. It is encouraging and wonderful to know that other people have the gift of sight and are able to share it openly with me. Here we were total strangers brought together on the day of the pope's arrival. The officer would never have seen me or James if not for the pope's visit. What an endearing experience. The day was filled with the heightened awareness surrounded in a mist of endless love.

Once Again James Protects Me

James told me in the 1970s that I would move to Florida. I thought, "No way. I love New York." But in the early 1990s, for family reasons, I moved from New York to Florida. Two days before I moved, as I came out of a store in downtown Brooklyn, James said to me: "Look up."

I looked up, but could not see anything. Then I felt as if James had put one of his hands on my shoulder, a signal he used in my conscious state to make sure I was paying attention and to stand still and observe. So I followed James's instruction and stayed where I was.

A few moments later, a man fell out of a nearby high-rise building and crashed onto the hard concrete. His brains and blood were splattered all over the sidewalk. Had I not been warned by James, I could have been killed by this crash.

I escaped this disaster thanks to James.

A Heartwarming Good-bye

I have several favorite songs. One is for Eileen, "When Irish Eyes Are Smiling," and for James, "Amazing Grace." Both songs are sung by those in an audience before I go into a full trance. Both Eileen and James adore when people sing those songs for them. My own special song is "Danny Boy." James and Eileen know how much I love the song "Danny Boy," especially when played by pipers from Ireland.

The day before I left for Florida, as I walked all the streets of my beloved Brooklyn Heights, committing everything to memory and recalling the fantastic times with friends and family, I said to myself, "I want to leave Brooklyn Heights with a memory that I will never forget."

As I was turning the corner from Montague Street, I saw

a lone bagpiper, dressed in a kilt with matching socks and cap, carrying his case with his pipes in it and looking for the right spot to perform. I could not believe this was happening. As I walked past him, mainly to make sure he was real and not something conjured up, he started playing. What was he playing? "Danny Boy"!

Realizing my wish had been granted, I stood there and cried. What a treat to remember Brooklyn Heights by.

Edgar Cayce's Migraine Headache Recipe

In the past, I suffered from migraine headaches. One day while writing a letter to a friend, I saw a strange thing from the spirit world enter my house. Part of an elbow attached to a white shirt glided past me and into another room in my house. This partial ghostly manifestation also came with a bad smell.

I said, "Oh, please go away, whoever you are. The smell is causing my eyes to water."

It was a very strong smell of liniment. The more I complained about the awful smell, the stronger it seemed. I remember jokingly saying, "Please take your stink and go."

Then I heard chuckling in my head and it was made known to me that Edgar Cayce was here.

Edgar Cayce was born in 1887 and passed away in 1945. With a reputation as the Sleeping Prophet, Cayce rendered more than fourteen thousand readings in his lifetime over a wide array of subject matter. Cayce delivered these discourses while he was lying down with his eyes closed, in an altered state of consciousness. He did not have any formal education in medicine, but he was able to describe individuals and diagnose their physical conditions with surprising accuracy, even though they may have been hundreds of miles away.

Cayce gave me a recipe to relieve my migraine. This method

is different from what he said when he was mortal. Therefore,
I would like to share it with the readers:

> Put one cup of castor oil and two cups of water in
> a saucepan. Bring the mixture to a boil, then cool
> it down a little bit. Add three white terry cloths (or
> washcloths) into the solution. Wring them till they
> no longer drip water. Find a comfortable place to
> lie down. Put one cloth over your eyes, one over
> your forehead, and one over the back of your neck.
> Keep doing this until you use up every ounce of the
> solution. Do it for fourteen days straight.

I followed that advice and have not had a headache for
many years.

Eat and Drink with the Spirits

James and Eileen, and on occasion June, often come to me
and ask if I will indulge in certain foods and beverages so they
can sense and perhaps even taste the foods through me. It is
always my pleasure to comply.

Occasionally, James asks me to eat a certain vegetable.
Since he does not have a physical body, he is not able to smell
or taste our food by himself, so he asks me to eat carrots,
string beans, and corn so he can taste the food through me. I
do not know how this works, but I do know, based on feedback
from James, that he is always delighted.

James also warned me more than thirty years ago to stop
eating shrimp. He says they are the scavengers of the waters
and thus when we eat them we can get sick from what they
have ingested. I try hard to avoid shrimp, but truly, it is one
of my favorite foods.

I once asked James if he had ever tasted ice cream. He had

never heard of this treat. So I ate some ice cream just for him. His reaction was good, and he said he loved it. Unfortunately for James I seldom eat ice cream because my throat has a bad reaction to it.

Eileen has exquisite taste in food as well as in clothes. Eileen likes to eat good food. She will not taste nor does she tolerate fast food, and she has told me she prefers me not to eat it. I sometimes used to go to a restaurant in Manhattan to eat fish cooked the way Eileen wished—sometimes baked and sometimes broiled. She also occasionally enjoyed a piece of bread from Balducci's or a tiny bit of dessert from Dean & Deluca. As for drinks, she likes to taste martinis through me.

I try to accommodate their wishes, but sometimes my stomach just does not cooperate.

One time in the 1980s, I was a guest at a lovely dinner party. In an elegantly designed dish was an array of tiny beads. I was watching as people put these beads on crackers and ate them. I had to show I was savvy, so I took a little dab and put some on a cracker. After taking a tiny nibble, I rushed myself into the nearest washroom and proceeded to chuck this stuff up.

I heard Eileen say, "Oh dear, have you never tasted caviar?"

I said, "No. Never."

Eileen teased me about not having developed the proper taste for certain foods.

I replied, "Since it isn't a requirement as part of working with the spirit as a medium, I shall never acquire a taste for eating fish eggs regardless how fancy or important this awful tasting treat is to many people. I don't think I will ever want to."

Driving with the Spirits

In addition to eating, I also have some driving experience with spirits. James has a classic name for automobiles—the *chariots*. He often says, "Let's get into your chariot."

One day in the late 1990s, I was driving on Florida State Road 7 (US Highway 441), which at the time had only two lanes. In order to pass a car, one had to change into the oncoming lane. A car could not easily go in front of another to pass, especially when other cars were coming in the opposite direction.

While I was driving, James suddenly warned me, "Turn your chariot."

I did not know which way James wanted me to turn. Then I felt James hold my hands and turn the steering wheel to the right. The whole action seemed as if the car had turned by itself. I recall my hands frozen to the steering wheel and the wheel turning of its own accord. At that moment, I noticed a car coming toward me at a very high speed. The driver tried to pass by turning into my lane. James somehow maneuvered me out of harm's way, and the oncoming car almost hit the truck behind me. Although this episode turned out well, it took a toll on my nerves and I pulled over to the side of the road to collect myself. The truck driver who had been behind me on the road was screaming at the other driver. She could have caused a very bad accident. It was James who saved me and took me through this fiasco. He does rescue me many times and in my opinion has saved me from potential deadly happenings.

Eileen also loves to go riding in my car, but does not care for driving it. She used to encourage me to drive. About nine years after I started driving, she confessed that she had had no taste for driving when she was mortal, but rather enjoyed being a passenger, and she didn't want me to pick up on that feeling.

She still has no desire to drive with me and prefers it to remain that way. But James loves to drive my chariot, and I often sense his hands on mine while driving the car.

Art Appreciation

Before I moved to Florida in the early 1990s, I used to go to the Metropolitan Museum of Art with my companion spirits James and Eileen and my dear friend Doris. We would try to do this at least once a month. To me, there is no place more exciting and beautiful than the Metropolitan Museum of Art.

James loved the Frank Lloyd Wright exhibit and marveled at the dynamic spatial continuity and the minimized distinction between inner and outer space.

Eileen favored the decorative glass by Louis Comfort Tiffany. She was especially attracted to the deep, vibrant hues radiating from the opalescent glasses. She also asked that I dress appropriately for the trip, because after our gushing over the magnificent art work, we would all more than likely wind up in the cafeteria to rest, relax, compare notes, express our opinions, watch people, and slowly sip a cup of cappuccino or a mug of hot chocolate. She asked me not to wear blue jeans and a plaid shirt, which was my usual city attire, so on weekends when going out with Doris and knowing that my spirit companions were coming with us, I made a special effort to wear nice clothes.

My favorite were the impressionists. Standing in front of the works of Monet, Renoir, and Pissarro, I was like a child let loose in a candy store. I would gaze at the works and forget the passage of time.

On several of these occasions another spirit joined us. He

stood with us for hours on end in front of the Cézanne exhibits. This spirit, which I would later learn was that of Ernest Hemingway, loved this man's art; so do I.

We all liked to see the architecture of churches. I have a passion to go into cathedrals, churches, or temples and gaze at the awesome interior structure. The smell of the old wood is so calming. I love the interiors and am always amazed how much good psychic work I accomplish in these places. Grace Church, Saint Patrick's Cathedral, and Saint Thomas's are among my favorite old jaunts in New York City.

I always got very excited about the Metropolitan Museum of Art and my favorite special churches. I believe they were somehow connected to my life deeply and felt they were extensions of me. These places bring me to total peace and harmony and the wonderful added part is that my beloved James and Eileen loved these trips as much as I did. I do miss going to these places very much.

When I visited the museum, I learned from James to enjoy the moment, to allow him to feel my happiness and joy while viewing the magnificent art.

Spirit Connected to Spirits

Sometimes spirits come near me because of James or Eileen.

One day a visitor came close to me. My sense of him was different from that of James or Eileen. He felt lighter of heart and much more playful. I thought I heard him say his name was Uvani. I questioned him for several minutes as to why he would visit me, since he is not my control. He was in fact Eileen's control when she was mortal and doing work as a trance medium.

I was intrigued by his presence, but slightly confused at the same time. Did this mean another level of opening would become a permanent part of my mediumistic development?

Eileen interceded and told me that she didn't know whether or not her own process of thought had created him for me. Then an odd feeling welled up deep in my solar plexus and got stronger the longer Uvani stayed with me. I felt a gentle but evident vibration with a tickling sensation in that region of my body. While this was going on, my mind kept drifting to a foreign land from ancient times. The weirdest thing was how easily I accepted Uvani and how, somewhere deep within me, it felt right for him to be with us. I felt as though his existence contained a part of me. When he came near, it felt as though I may have owned his arms and legs. It felt like we were connected, through a different way; unlike when Eileen and James came to me, where I feel and sense them and they take over my body, this was the reverse—not necessarily through speaking, but more like flesh-to-flesh transformation.

There was a lot of chuckling attached to this episode. Perhaps it was, as Eileen said, just a visit from her old friend that she may have thought about and created for me. I guess he had enough fun with me, because after a while as the sensations stopped, it felt like a wall was put over my eyes so I could not see.

In the early 1970s, when my daughter was severely ill with an asthma attack, and I thought I would lose her, I called for James and other spirits who might be nearby to please help my little girl. I expected someone like James or Edgar Cayce to help me, or if not one of them, at least some spirit of great ancient American healers or English doctors. Instead, a spirit clad in a foreign costume came to me. He whispered, "Your little girl will live."

I said, "Thank you very much. Who are you?"

The spirit said, "U-Vi. You will get to know me better."

I asked, "What does that mean?"

He said, "It means light. I bring the light."

I said, "Can you bring the healing with the light?"

He just gently moved away.

At another time, I asked to bring in any doctor in heaven to come to save my daughter. Another spirit came. He was a tall figure and gave off a slightly greenish cast about him. His ghostly manifestation was wearing a dark, long, elegant robe with jewels on it. For a second I thought he was a Chinese doctor. He turned around and said, "Just place your hand on her chest. Keep it there gently."

I did and it felt like an electric shock went through my right hand. About six hours later, my daughter felt better. I cannot say her recovery was because of the spirit, but I can attest that the experience existed.

I asked him, "Who are you?"

He did not answer at that time. But years later, when I was very ill, he came and told me his name was Abdul.

I believe my first encounters with Uvani and Abdul came to me when I asked for help in the 1970s. I also believe that they stayed near me because Eileen, whose identity had not yet been revealed to me, had been their medium.

My enormous thanks and gratitude go to these wonderful, caring souls. All five play very important roles in attempts to keep me—and all those close to me—healthy and aware. I am deeply indebted to June, James, and Eileen and her guests, Uvani and Abdul.

On many other occasions, I would invoke the healing powers from James, who strictly uses his ancient Kabala sounds to enter and heal us. This, too, works little healing miracles. I have firsthand experience with my beloved James's healing abilities. They have seldom failed to help.

Einstein Returned

When I stopped automatic writing in the early 1990s, I thought I had lost the capability to communicate with the spirits and felt an overwhelming loss. Thoughts swirled in my mind about them no longer wanting me to do this work. I missed the daily ritual of writing with James and Eileen, which had become the familiar way of communicating.

I said to the spirits, "This is terrible. Why have you forsaken me? What did I do? What did I do that was wrong?"

I felt rejected and remembered how I had initially rejected them, and then finally accepted them. Now they were rejecting me. I felt sad at best.

I was frustrated for several weeks because the spirits did not come through automatic writing, and every attempt I made to do this with them failed. At that time, I did not understand that a new stage had begun and that a new way of learning was in the works. It took a while, but eventually I realized that I was not forsaken. My visions had been getting sharper and sharper over the years, and perhaps it was time to do other things with the spirits and put to rest the daily ritual of writing.

As this new thought entered my mind, I became calmer and looked forward to whatever new things the spirits had in store. I am always eager to learn and grow from my experiences so that I can share with others and they may in turn learn, grow, and share. To my relief, I smelled the myrrh again. I was told clearly, "Go to the library."

I went to the library. I was looking around and was led by the spirits down to a section of psychology books. I did not understand what I was looking for. I was looking up and down under the books, getting dizzy from all the bending. Then a man approached me and said, "You're the psychic."

I said, "I beg your pardon?"

He said, "Well, my spirit guide told me I'd meet you here."

I thought I would drop dead in the library. I asked him, "Who's your spirit guide?"

"Well, Einstein. Albert Einstein."

I thought, "Yeah, right." But then I laughed to myself, thinking, "Well, wait a minute. I walk with James. How am I any different?"

It turned out that he lived in Brooklyn Heights and was a scientist who studied quantum mechanics and unified theory. He was a professor at Long Island University. His mother had recently passed away and left him a good sum of money, so he did not have to work.

He said he had to meet another person on a journey like this and he was told that he would be comforted by my words. My control entity, on the other hand, had not given me any of that information.

Now, as I look back, I understand that James wanted to teach me that I could have faith and question at the same time. I needed to have faith in knowing that I was supposed to meet this scientist. If I had been given clear directions, I would have understood that I was supposed to be there to meet somebody who was going to approach me because we were on the same wavelength. But no detailed explanations had been given to me.

The professor and I were friends for about three months. Although I am not a scientist, I was able to talk to this man. I understood everything he told me. He showed me things that his spirit guide led him to and we would converse on the theory of unavailable energy. My ability to carry a smooth conversation shocked both of us.

He was able to accept the spirit communication that was

taking place with him in a much shorter amount of time than I had.

He believed that he went to other planets in his dream states. He described to me the aliens he had seen: "They're really all around. You just have to sense them."

I asked him if he communicated with them. He said he communicated with them in mathematical ways or with musical notes.

After a while, he became difficult for me to communicate with because I am more inclined to deal with the here and now and what is going on in our world, how we can help others as well as ourselves, how the spirits can help us, and what lessons we are supposed to learn. It was hard for me to swallow his meeting and speaking with aliens. But it put me in a peculiar spot to even mention that thought, because how dare I rebuke his work? Was what I do any less hard to swallow? I let him know that I could appreciate what he was going through and that he was not alone in this world doing what he was doing, just like I am not alone.

I believe that the spirits wanted me to have this encounter so I would know that I was not alone and that there were perhaps hundreds or thousands of people like me out there. Our paths will meet and we might be comforted. We have a responsibility with what is being given to us, and we must share it and teach others so that they can open their inner awareness, too.

My friend mentioned that he met and spoke to Einstein as if the experience was flesh to flesh.

I asked, "Will you be able to finish Einstein's unfinished equation on the unified theory?"

He said, "No, it is not important. The Japanese will finish it."

I asked him, "What is the most important lesson that Einstein taught you?"

He said, "Enjoy your mortal life."

Back then I could not understand it. But now, as I am getting older, I think I do. We have to live for now, plan a little bit for tomorrow. But most of all, we must know that life continues and enjoy our lives. If you can bring happiness and health to others, then help others. I believe that is what someone like Einstein would have wanted.

Grandfather's Visit

My grandfather Sam and I had a special bond. I attribute my entire opening up into the world of psychic/mediumship to him. Everything I do in this field goes back to my youth. *It started with Grandpa.*

On a snowy winter day in the 1980s, I took a nasty fall on some ice that was hidden by fresh snow, and my knees and ankle were hurt. The fall left me in a wobbly condition, but I was still able to walk further until I reached the building where I lived.

As I have noted before, the elevators often broke down, and why should this particular day be any exception, especially when I once again needed one to get me up to the twentieth floor?

With many packages under my arm, I dreaded the thought of walking up all those flights. My knees and ankle would never allow me to make it. I waited for about ten minutes and somehow got lost in listening to other people's conversations about the hardship of having no elevator service. Then my grandfather's voice became loud in my head, saying to me, "We always walked. We always walked. You can do it. Start walking."

It took all these years for Grandpa to come for a visit! I was excited and eager to do what he asked. I cannot recall how I managed to go up twenty flights with a fresh injury, lugging packages, but do know we did it, Grandpa and me. I only remember the sheer delight in knowing he was beside me and encouraging me to continue.

When I entered my apartment, I was greeted by the sweet smell of the tobacco he had always used in his pipe. I felt embraced by his aroma and soothed by his presence.

What is amazing to me is that he never came to give advice or offer to stay with my family for a while. He did not even tell me how he was doing or what things he had learned in his new state of being.

His visit was very short but dearly appreciated. I never heard from him again, yet an inner knowing says he is never too far. When I asked James why my grandfather came and left so quickly, he said that during my dream states I kept calling out for him and it was decided that a sweet visit was appropriate. Thank you very much, dear James. When I asked how I felt little to no pain from the accident, James said he put invisible bandages on me. I like that.

Grandpa came and went. Although his visit was brief, it was also very endearing and added yet more proof that life continues.

Grandmother's Visit

My grandmother was far advanced for a peasant woman. She had tons of wisdom. To me, she was all heart and all happiness. She was the one who told me she loved me every day in my life.

Ever since my grandmother passed away at age eighty-six, I have felt that her spirit is around, but it does not come with any particular aroma. I am careful with the subtle differences. You have to be able to learn the differences when sensing spirits among what you are dreaming, what you are thinking, or what you wish to happen. When my grandmother came, I sensed more than I smelled. I just sensed she was near.

Although my grandfather was a tailor and my grandmother used her machine on a daily basis, I cannot even sew a straight line. I get frustrated and cry whenever I am in front of a machine or when I have to sit down with a needle and thread. When my grandmother was alive, she used to help me sew and had so much patience in showing me how to use the sewing machine.

One day in the early 1980s, while I was trying to sew with the sewing machine, I mentally said, "Grandma, I wish you were near me to help me sew a straight line."

As soon as I thought this, I felt a tap on my shoulder. I knew it was my grandmother—when she was living, she would often tap me on my shoulder to signal "Just keep at it" or "Job well done."

Her visit was also brief, but reminded me that patience is important when using a sewing machine.

Sometimes Grandma would come to me in my dream states and take me on journeys to places she enjoyed staying. Her favorite place was a farm that had many cows and a few goats. I was glad to know her love for animals continued and she was happy enjoying her farm life.

Mother's Near-Death Experience

My mother never knew about my communication with Eileen and James. As I said earlier, she and my grandmother endured so much with me during my younger years that I truly felt I needed to spare her of all else that went on regarding the paranormal. Both of them were so very good to me.

When my mother was seriously ill and hospitalized for several weeks in the mid-1990s, I spent between five and seven hours every day at the hospital with her. She lapsed in and out of a coma. Although she could barely talk, I decided to try an experiment with her.

While she was in the coma state, I sat upon her bed and started to talk. At first I spoke of our family, her grandchildren, and happy times that we all shared. Then I talked of what was going on in the world and read some articles from the newspaper. During the first two weeks she never once stirred, but I refused to give up hope. Since I had already spoken of events of the living, I decided I would try to steer our one-sided conversation in a different direction that would involve her if she were at all able to respond to me. I realized nothing may come of it, but at that time I needed to explore avenues that are considered far out there.

Sitting on her bed, I began to sing "When Irish Eyes Are Smiling."

My mother never opened her eyes, but she started to talk to me. She said, "Marilyn, I see you."

I said, ""But your eyes are closed, Mom."

She said, "I see you here."

I said, "Where is here?"

And she answered, "You're standing across the river."

"What river?" I asked.

She said, "It's not a water river. It's wavy shimmering light that expands across a wide span and the only word I have for it is 'river.'"

I said, "Oh, OK. Now where are you?"

She said, "I'm with Daddy."

I said, "Do you like it there?"

She said, "Very much. It's very, very beautiful."

"Marilyn," my mother continued, "you're with two very nice people."

I asked, "Oh, who are these people?"

She replied, "I have no idea, but they seem to really stick to you, and the man has his hands on your shoulders."

My mother had never known about my communication with Eileen and James, nor who they were or what they looked like.

I said to my mother, "Ma, ask the man his name."

My mother said, "I think he's calling himself Jacob."

At this point, I started to get very excited, but I had to keep reminding myself that my mother was in a light coma with her eyes closed while having a conversation with me about my beloved spirit James.

Mom continued, "I am not clear on his name. He may be saying Jake or Jakov, but I think it is Jacob."

"Really?" I was amazed; actually, more in mild, happy shock.

"Yeah, that's what he said. Jacob."

I kept questioning her, "Who's the lady, Ma?"

My mother had never heard me mention Eileen but she said confidently, "That's easy. Her name is Eileen."

"Does she have a last name?"

She said, "She's yelling out 'Garrett.'"

I was immensely impressed with what was going on. At points in our conversation my mother's voice grew weaker, so I bent over her body so I could hear her.

I said, "What did the man and the lady tell you?"

"They're telling me I'm going to be OK and that soon I'm going to be here forever. But that you're going to be OK because they're going to be with you for your forever."

I said, "How do you feel about that?"

She said, "I think it's going to be OK. They seem awfully nice, Marilyn."

I said, "Thank you, Ma. Do you want to wake up now?"

She said, "I am up, silly."

I said, "But your eyes are still closed."

She said, "It's not time for me to cross the river yet."

Then, about three hours later, her eyes opened and she was awake until the day she went back into another light coma and passed away. During those two months, dementia started to set in, and I asked her, "Ma, do you remember the story you told me about Jacob and Eileen?" And she said, "Who are they?"

When my mother was moved to a nursing home for her final days with us, another interesting thing happened.

I had asked of whatever powers that be to please allow my mom to die in my arms. I considered this a gift. Three days before my mother died, Eileen had said to me, "Stay in the nursing home. Do not leave her side." When I needed to take a shower, Eileen instructed me to just run home to take a shower and come right back. So I did what she said. I would rush going and coming for fear of her leaving without saying good-bye.

On the second day, nothing happened, but I spoke with the staff and made sure my mother was given the proper dosage of medication to help alleviate the severe pains in her leg.

On the third day, Eileen said, "Marilyn, tonight is the night. Stay very close."

I did not leave my mother's side, even for a minute. I held my mother in my arms and sang to her. Through crying jags and with a very heavy heart, I kept singing songs that she used to hum to me in my youth. While crying like a baby, I tried hard to remember all her favorite songs. Although I couldn't remember the words to most of the songs, I still hummed and continued until the end.

In between humming and crying, I was trying to tell her she was going to be OK, that most of her family and friends would greet her, and mostly how much I loved her and how honored I was to be her daughter.

A very short time before her passing, my younger daughter felt the need to visit along with a friend of the family. Then a cousin of ours also felt the need to come but could not explain the urgency. The three of them were overwhelmed when they saw my mother cradled in my arms as I was singing to her. I held her in my arms until she went cold from the bottom up. Thank you, Eileen and James, for granting my wish to be with my mother during her passing.

Mother's Visit from Beyond

After my mother passed away, as I was busy doing laundry and sorting out her clothes, the strong aroma of her body was near. I said, "Mom, show me more."

Within a few seconds, the back of my left palm had water spots on it. I gently put my tongue to these spots. They were salty. Until this day, I believe they were the tears of my mother. I said "Thank you" and asked her to please stay and to visit me often.

I did not receive any signal from her for several months. I complained to James, "I could speak for the whole world. All the other people have their mommies and daddies coming through. I don't even see or sense her. I don't even feel her. I feel hurt. Where is my mother?"

A few days passed without any answer to my question. Then one evening, I was lying down in bed, just beginning to doze off. I felt something in the bed next to me. I turned to look, and there was my mom, dressed in a 1940s-style tailored brown suit with high heels and nylons, and a figure like Bette Davis. She looked to be about forty years old.

I was excited and I said to her, "I must be dreaming. I must be dreaming."

She said, "Silly, I am in your dream now." And she took me by the hand and said, "Marilyn, I want you to come with me. But let that gentleman behind you put his hands on your shoulders so you don't get lost."

"OK."

"We have to go outside so make sure you put your slippers on," she said. "Listen carefully to what I tell you. Now I want you to close your eyes and I want you to free your mind of clutter. We will be going at a very fast speed, so keep holding my hand till I tell you it is OK to let go."

I was so happy, excited, and eager—and mostly thrilled to see my mother.

She continued, "Free yourself."

With the roaring sound of wind in my ears and the heavy smell of horse dung, off we went until we arrived at her special place in heaven.

I remember thinking that the loud roaring sound was getting even louder as we jettisoned further away from my mortal body. All the while, James held on to my shoulders so I would not fly off.

My mother showed me where she lived. I told her, "Oh, mom, this is fantastic. It looks like Brooklyn."

She replied, "I love it."

"But it looks similar to where you always lived."

"I love it," she repeated. "That's exactly what I want for now."

I noticed that all the people looked as if in their forties. I commented about this discovery to my mother: "How boring."

"Not really," she said. "I could choose to be twenty, forty, or seventy."

"Wow!"

"Now are you happy? Do you see I'm OK? It may take many more years before I visit you again, so keep all this memory," she told me.

"Where's Daddy?" I asked.

"Oh, I didn't want him to live in my house now," she said.

"Really?"

"Absolutely. I'm perfectly happy doing this alone."

As I came back, I did not see lights or tunnels. The same roaring sounds came back, along with the smell of horse dung and the sensation of walking on lots of wet grass. The next day I woke up and found that I had left a trail of grass and mud on my back porch, which I had also tracked into the house. My porch screen door was opened and there was evidence that I must have been outdoors. Otherwise, how did all the grass and mud tracks get into my house leading to my bedroom? I was amazed by this trace of evidence because I did not remember being outside of my house or opening the porch door. I am not a sleepwalker.

☙ ☙ ☙

My interaction with the spirits has given me fascinating experiences with others in both the spirit world and the physical world. From the living people in the modern world to whom my spirit friends have guided me, to the spirits of everyday people who lived long ago and the spirits of those who were close to me in this life—each of these encounters is like a miraculous nutrient, which makes my life fuller and richer, like rare dye that keeps my life always newly colorful.

7

Sharing the Knowledge

Every action of our lives touches on some chord that will vibrate in eternity.
                    —Edwin Hubbel Chapin (1814–1880)

EVERYTHING I CAN do is teachable, and that means if you discipline yourself to study the many different aspects of paranormal studies, then you will have success at it. This is no different from learning any other subject matter that requires your full attention. It also means that by trial and error you will become capable of learning where your strengths and weaknesses are. I often tell my students to work hard and discipline themselves, and to keep at it on a daily basis. The rewards will eventually show, and the satisfaction of doing this work will be great, especially when your *hits* are greater than your *misses*.

Everyone can learn about inner awareness and everyone is certainly capable of becoming very good at it. People must train themselves to have clarity of mind, sincerity, and a heart filled with trust and love, in order to grow. When we grow, our society as a whole will improve and mankind will be elevated to a higher and better level of maturity, love, compassion, understanding, and peace. With this belief, I started teaching psychic development in the late 1970s.

I have never advertised my classes, but many people have become aware of them. I used the "round robin" telephone method of getting the news out about a class. I usually called only three people, asking them to each invite one or two others, but we somehow always ended up with more than the twelve to fifteen I considered ideal for this type of gathering. Some Saturday nights more than thirty or forty people would show up, gathering in a small apartment somewhere in Brooklyn, Queens, or Manhattan to take part in a psychic development class. Because we often lacked chairs for everyone, it was not uncommon for people to sit on the floor. When there was no space, we would open the front door to the apartment and allow participants to sit in the hallway. I could not make all the people comfortable, so it was understood that those with medical problems would be given chairs to sit on. Somehow we managed.

Many of my students came from great distances away and had to struggle to find parking. Many traveled by bus or subway, which was not an easy feat. Yet they came. Our classes were made up of people from all walks of life, and many different professions, including doctors, lawyers, homeopaths, teachers, and writers. We all got along in spite of our diverse backgrounds and economic status.

My workshops lasted four to five hours and we did experiments and exercises in all areas pertaining to paranormal studies. Great emphasis was put upon telepathy, psychometry, aura reading, meditation, table tipping, dowsing, healing, altered states of consciousness, astral travel, and mediumistic work. Sometimes I would offer only two or three subject areas, for instance, telepathy, psychometry, and aura reading. For this type of class I had my students focus intensely on these areas. We spent hours doing exercises in each area.

People were often amazed at how easy it was to open up to their own psychic ability. It was and still is a joy for me to witness the unfolding of my students' talents. Everyone has a gift in some area. When the right buttons are pushed, magic will take place. However, it usually takes more than just going to classes for one to reach his or her potential. People need to study and work at it. They must not treat this subject matter lightly and walk away from it when they become bored or when they feel nothing is happening. Patience is important, along with determination and discipline to keep at to develop your skills. Some people have a natural talent, but this does not mean that the skills cannot be taught.

Before coming to my class, some of my students had read books pertaining to the many different subject areas in this field. Others had personal experiences they wanted to explore, and several had no previous experience, but their curiosity was so great that they needed to seek answers that would allow them to balance their daily lives with the nagging curiosity that would not go away.

Some of these people were very gifted, while many were not. It truly did not matter. The bottom line is that if you stick with it, you will catch up to what others can seemingly do without effort. Most people have wonderful spontaneous events and are not aware that with proper training one can make most of these occurrences happen on a regular basis. Some people had experiences of hearing voices. Some came with a hope for helping themselves find answers to live a better quality of life, almost like a passion one needs in redeeming belief.

I tell my students, "We start everybody as equal. We start

all the same, regardless of how many classes you go to. Let's see what we can do." As a teacher, I feel it incumbent upon me to make all my students comfortable, regardless of their gifts and knowledge. All must get along with each other, and everyone must be supportive and sensitive to each other in all my classes. I will not tolerate childish behavior or negativity in any way, shape, or form. I believe it is important to allow students to shine and blossom in whatever area they find themselves comfortable in. For some it is mediumistic work; for others it is strictly using their psychic ability. Others are able to find they can do a smattering of many different aspects and enjoy the variety of areas they have become proficient at. With a good measure of encouragement and gentleness, most of my students are eager to learn and get excited when their abilities start to shine.

Many people would bring me all kinds of music recordings that purport to offer instant relaxation, because they thought that I could use them when I teach. Or they would come to me saying, "Oh, I listen to this music and it puts me in a lovely state of mind." Some would bring incense, color charts, or other items they felt helped them reach certain levels of relaxation. They all meant well and certainly are entitled to their beliefs, but I put everything brought to our classes aside, and often found myself faced with the challenge of having to discourage them from tainting others in my group who were new to this field and needed to learn to conquer their thoughts and emotions and build their confidence without the aid of such tools. I have always felt that the person is the tool, and that everyone, regardless of ability, need only to use their minds to establish terrific results while doing this work. In my opinion, people should become more aware that they do not need music, cards, or other items offered to help them coddle themselves while learning how to do psychic work.

Regrettably, most of my peers do not feel as I do and insist that outside help is important in the development of one's talents. To me, the person is the gift. That's why I spend hours giving workshops so people can explore, experiment, and expand their natural and learned talents by using their own techniques—without the use of outside materials. As politely as possible I ask my students to keep their treasures away from the class. If they feel the need to share what has worked for them, they can discuss it during our ten-minute breaks or contact others outside class time. I am careful here to say that I am not saying my way or no way, but in fact am saying I prefer to stick to the format I use because music, color wheels, incense, and other items can be offensive to others and cause too many distractions.

My classes are inclusive; they are not for those who solely want to meditate, nor for only a select few, nor for those who wish to push their ways upon others. Many years ago a lady came to class with sage, expecting me to light it. When I refused, she got offended, accusing me of not caring for the spirits, who love and need sage. Needless to say I held my tongue until after class, when I called this ignorant lady. I told her that she must continue in her belief, but asked her to stay away from my classes because if I allowed her to try to force her beliefs onto others, only she and other sage users would grow.

I tell all my students to please not wear perfumes, toilet water, or aftershave lotions, or bring candles, incense, or other items that have aromas to any of my classes because they could trigger a severe allergy in many of us, making us distracted while we waste time taking care of our coughs and sneezes. I also tell the hostess of whichever house we gather at to please help me enforce this rule.

Another, more sensitive thing I ask my students to do before entering my class is to park their religion at the front door and pick it up on the way out.

Many religions prohibit their followers from exploring the world of spirits or psychic matters and have gone so far to deem such behavior as dancing with the devil. I have no room in my teachings for dealing with people who are grappling with what their church deems the corruption of their soul, and thus I refuse to allow such thoughts to contaminate my students. The environment in which I teach must be free to explore everything, free of the burden of people thinking they are dwelling in hell or sinning.

So I politely ask students to please not use their religion in any manner that would reflect negatively upon our studies. Many of my students are devout Roman Catholics and, although they need to explore their gifts, it is extremely hard for them to come to grips with what their church deemed evil and what they had to learn and grow with. Several of them came once, then never returned. The bottom line is: *When you come to my class, you have to park your religion at the front door, along with all the other items, and pick it up on your way out.*

Another thing I ask of my students is that if they are being treated for an emotional or mental disorder to please ask their medical professional if coming to a class like mine is appropriate and, if possible, to ask their doctor to join us or call me so that everything is understood beforehand, and all the possible risks are taken care of.

In addition, I insist that no one come to my class if they are using alcoholic beverages or self-medicating on other drugs. My classes are not to be used as a platform for people who are dependent upon drugs or for those who feel they can share fantasies and delusions and attempt to pass them off as truth to others who simply came to learn and grow. I have seen too many people fool others, and sadly many of my students have been taken in by such nonsense, much of which is either pure fantasy or outright lies. It is up to me, their teacher, to keep our environment free from those who might pollute it.

James and Eileen's Participation

In the 1970s, 1980s, and early 1990s, I taught psychic development classes throughout Brooklyn, Queens, and Manhattan. In some of those classes, my beloved James told me that he would put me in a light altered state of consciousness so that he and Eileen would be able to speak through me to my students. I trust James with my life and certainly felt that if he needed to do this, then it would be wonderful for my students to witness firsthand what a trance medium is involved with and to observe how carefully the spirit control takes on responsibility for the medium. And since so many people fear going under and releasing their mind to another, witnessing this helped many budding mediums/channelers to overcome some of their fears.

Most of these trance states were much deeper than I expected. In fact, upon awakening, whole segments of time were lost to me, and I had no memory of what had taken place.

Since I was not aware of what took place, some of my students recorded these classes and gave me a copy of the recording. On many occasions, my friend Rita was kind enough to take notes so I would have a rough copy of the evening's discussion with the spirits. The written version was sometimes quite different from the taped session. We laughed at those differences, but the bottom line is that at the very least, I understood the gist of those sessions. To this day I find it curious that what we think we hear is often different from what is actually spoken.

Amazingly, even though I had no idea what transpired when James and Eileen had conversations with my students, the continuity of the evening was never broken. My students were delighted to be given such a treat. Most of them said they were in awe of meeting James and Eileen and that the information given was precious to their lives. I am happy to report that the benefit of what the spirits had to share with them on a direct and personal level was important and certainly outweighed my level of unawareness during the sessions.

I prepared myself for such an event by fasting a whole day. I fasted because the spirits told me it was easier to speak through me when my stomach was empty, and it avoided the problem of thoughts on my part about my digestion interfering or my body making sounds that I had no control over. I have been told that when they spoke, the room was so quiet that you could literally hear a pin drop. Preparing myself physically was part of my personal learning about the mechanics of being a medium. After each trance session, I would still gain as much as five to ten pounds of body weight. It seems that I accumulated a lot of water in my body, but I have no idea where the extra water came from. Usually it took about three days to get rid of the extra water weight.

While working in New York City, I did not drive or travel alone, so I was not concerned about the dizziness and slight disorientation that happens after every séance. However, when I moved down to Florida and learned how to drive, it became imperative to curtail the active involvement of James and Eileen unless someone else would be driving me to and from a session. To this day, when my work involves formal séances, I require someone else to drive me in both directions.

Before I enter the trance state, I like to hear the crowd sing "When Irish Eyes Are Smiling" to help me relax and welcome Eileen. Eileen once told me that if I needed some grounding before I went into a trance, then she would like to hear that song, partly because she was Irish and likes that song very much, but also because when people sing it, they tend to become more relaxed and offer up smiles, which definitely have a soothing effect upon all.

While the song is sung, I feel the sensation of a gentle tingling, sort of like a light vibration throughout my body, and then I no longer hear the singing voices. I feel like I am entering a loving space, somewhere very serene, without a care in the world. When the séance is over, I am brought back to consciousness moments before I am completely awake, so I often hear and retain the last few seconds of the conversation.

When the spirits come through, they not only talk through me but also alter part of my appearance. They also tend to change my posture in certain ways so as to make themselves feel a little more comfortable. For example, I have been told that when James comes through, I appear shorter and more muscular. My face looks wider, and people have told me that my head seems shrunken to my neck. James always uncrosses my legs. He talks with a lower pitch. James always sits; he never stands up or walks.

Eileen speaks through me using a higher pitch. However, when she is getting ready to speak, she sits in the classic female position with my legs crossed.

Eileen has also been known to move my body. She literally gets up—using my body—and walks us from one end of a room to another. I often ask my students if she ever stumbles or bumps into things. I find it an incredible feat for someone to take my body and move it about while my eyes are closed and I am unaware of what is going on.

James has had several past lifetimes as a Roman Catholic priest, due in part to his devotion to his brother Yeshua. Therefore, James is familiar with archaic Latin in addition to ancient Aramaic and ancient Hebrew. When he first came through me, he spoke using lots of phrases in those ancient tongues, primarily archaic Latin. Unfortunately, no one understood him. Then he talked in Old English, which at that point in our shared time together was his most modern language. Still, no one understood him.

Often, when James and Eileen speak at the same séance, she follows up after James has spoken and explains: "Just because you're a spirit doesn't mean you know the language of the room. You may know what the thoughts of those present are, but that does not preclude that you can speak their language, and that's why this type of (trance) mediumship is very different from (conscious) channeling: This kind of mediumship presents to the audience a shadow of who we were from a period of time in that mortal existence that we are sharing with you and speaking to you from. Sometimes it requires interpreters or people to listen carefully so they can enjoy the nuances of our past existence and also learn to appreciate that we are attempting to offer different aspects of ourselves. Not all mediumistic work is the same, as most of you are by now very much aware of."

When I heard this explanation from a taped copy of a séance, I felt very humble and honored, and to this day am very much in awe of my beloved James and Eileen.

Teaching—and Learning from—James

My sensing tells me that James has incorporated some of his thoughts with mine. This has been ongoing over the course of many years. I can tell when he is pushing a thought into my consciousness. For example, he might guide me toward a book in the library or move my feet in another direction so I ultimately avoid danger, or he might invade my concentration to make me pay attention to something that requires more focus. Sometimes he pulls me quickly out of harm's way and I know without a doubt that those occurrences are his doing, not mine—as, for example, when he grabbed hold of my steering wheel and saved me from a head-on collision and, of course, the many times in New York City when he moved me away from danger. Other times I hear his thoughts in my mind when he tells me to stay put and look to the north or up in the sky to catch a glimpse of a fading rainbow, or to quietly stand still in my backyard and watch the doves gather. The information he gives me is endless and all these interactions are expressions of love and kindness, and it works both ways: from the spirit to me, and from me to the spirit. Yes, we do have a love fest going on, as it should be.

When James blends his thoughts with mine, I am in the open state of mind of consciousness, which means I am fully awake and know what is going on. When I need James to express himself using modern English, I silently tell him to listen to how the people on the street are speaking. In the 1970s I would play radio shows during the day and in the evenings would have the TV on so he could become familiar with our language, and hopefully be able to see through my eyes or sense through his own special awareness things pertaining to our world as it existed during that time. I wanted to share our American culture, which included all the good things and some of the bad, too. Thus humor, sadness, wittiness, silliness, happiness, the brightest and slowest, intellectuals as well as stupid people, from the savvy and sophisticated to the dull and boring—all were on my list to show James. It came down to James to learn our American English language. Knowing that James was learning our expressions and mannerisms and the way certain words were used, I would listen to Bob Grant, who offered terrific debates on the radio, or watch thought-provoking shows like Ted Koppel's *Nightline*. I also had him watch shows like *The David Frost Show*, *Hawaii Five-O*, *Happy Days*, *Highway to Heaven*, *Star Trek*, and *Welcome Back, Kotter*. We also watched old movies like Laurel and Hardy, the Three Stooges, *The Grapes of Wrath*, and *Casablanca*. On Christmas Eve, I would watch the Vatican to keep him up to date.

Learning American English became quite a job; it did not just stop at turning on a TV or listening to a radio. James let me know that he could learn my language better by hearing my words and those around me. I would go to the library. I would read newspapers. I would read books so I could show him, page by page, how the words are written. I would make sure to read aloud so he could hear how the words were spoken. He told me that there would come a time when he would bring to us a great writer who was interested in and intrigued by the free use of our modern way of language. Little did I know then that it was to be Ernest M. Hemingway. So, in usual sharing fashion, I said my thank you and we continued sharing the American way of speaking.

In the late 1990s, when vulgarity and freer use of what were once considered dirty words became an ordinary language as part of many TV shows, I must admit I felt ashamed that our society was losing respect and had unleashed an anything-can-be-spoken-of attitude. James took it all in stride and thought that we, as an ever-evolving species, had come a very long way. He did not feel ashamed but in fact thought it was wonderful to see our world forge onward toward a more intelligent, wiser society, unencumbered by judgment of the words people use. He explained that in order to grow we all must shed the shackles that hold us back, and that what may sound awful to people in my age group for a period of time is really nothing more than a long journey to ultimately becoming a freer, more intelligent human society, even if at first glance it means so-called dirty language is overused. He noted that as our society evolves, these expressions will fade and be replaced by other words that will impart much greater meaning than our present-day use of dirty words.

This is amazing to me, as to this day I blush when I hear dirty words used to express an ordinary occurrence, yet my beloved James finds it acceptable and by no means something to get bent out of shape about.

Although I have not yet come to the same level of acceptance as James has, it is funny when you think of the vocabulary we use today. When I was growing up, the use of curse words, or what we called the "dirty words," was never allowed. I remember using "crap"—still an awful word to say—in place of the "S word." Until about ten years ago, as our society freed up the usage of the no-no words, I was very hung up on hearing people utter them. When I was a kid, my mother admonished me severely for saying, "Oh damn." My concern was also what the spirits might think of us when they hear words like "damn," "bitch," or the dreaded "F word." It used to be a dilemma, but since James explained that it did not bother him or anyone else in the spirit realm, I feel less ashamed, but still somewhat embarrassed.

As James improved his verbal communication, many people were able to understand his wit, dry humor, and predictions.

During one session, James spoke of the plane crash of Pan Am flight 103. A student listened to this and contacted a friend on the West Coast who was scheduled for that flight and subsequently changed her plans. Other things he spoke of included the beginning and the end of the Gulf War, the shooting of President Ronald Reagan, World Series victories for the Mets and the Yankees, events in the stock market, and so on. He covered a wide variety of things that were important to those of us living between the 1970s and the 1990s. And he also told of things far off into the future, such as the future transformation of world religions eight hundred years to come. But he also made it clear that he did not enjoy being used as a forecaster of future events.

During another session, James directly told several students to stop being lazy. He offered them methods to help them open up and improve their skills. He also gave them hope. It warmed my heart when students would tell me how James or Eileen helped them to find a focus in their quest and to better understand the journey they were on.

He encouraged us to open our hearts and receive his words with love. He explained the meaning of "faith" and how it must be applied to all lives. Faith means work, and the two must go together. In his mortal life, James belonged to a religious sect he called Essenes. I later learned that "Essenes" means "doers of Torah." That is probably why James places so much emphasis on work.

One day in the 1990s, James said through my trance state that he would speak in an ancient Aramaic language he used when he lived as Ya'akov bar Yosef. Then he started saying some ancient Aramaic words. At the end of each trance session, James chants a blessing in ancient Aramaic to the sitters or the students in attendance.

James speaks with a deep passion in a booming voice. He understands the challenges facing those who try to accept what he had to say. Most audiences are in shock after hearing what he has to share, mainly because it conflicts with what is written in the Bible.

James directed our focus to things pertaining to ancient Qumran, the role he played in service of the Hebrews during the days of Yeshua, how his family lived in the Essene community, what the political and religious climate was, and how his life came to an end. As the second son in a devout Hebrew family, who loved and followed Yeshua completely, James makes it quite clear what his mission in life was and still is. James states that he wrote extensively about his brother Yeshua and First Temple/Church. He often tells the class that his purpose was to offer love through his teachings of his brother, and he wanted everyone to embrace him. He describes in detail the events that led up to his own death, and who was behind it. He is bombarded with questions and answers all with information that includes dates, names, events, and what role, if any, the questioner played during those times. He says that much of his written work is yet to be found and translated. He goes on to tell that when his writings are found, it will have a positive impact on people of all religions, and that his writings are intellectual enough for modern man to appreciate the times in which he wrote. Many will love his work; others will not. He hopes to enlighten and help ease the controversy over what truly happened to his brother and the rest of his family during and shortly after the times of Yeshua. He further adds that the enlightenment he speaks of will take place in the twenty-first century.

In one of my classes, he told a student that he had been a Sadducee and an important man in the Temple of the Hebrews, and another that she had been a mother who fled to the mountaintop with her children during the terror reign of the Romans.

On several occasions, he brought his mother, Miriam to visit with us. After these visits, I came out of a deep trance and looked at the faces staring at me. There was hardly a dry eye in the audience. Everyone seemed to be in their own special place, as if they too were in the grip of a trance. Some were in awe. I was told that my body had a light bluish color surrounding it while Miriam spoke of Yeshua and James. To this day, James primarily discusses matters referring to his sojourn on earth with his brother Yeshua.

During my private time with him, we have had discussions referring to Old Wisdom, especially with regard to Sophia, who brings the heart of the Supreme Being alive. He mentioned Sophia and Hokmah[1] in one thought, and I must admit heavy confusion set in. I knew it was important to inquire further, but he asked me not to fuss over it at that point in time, explaining that when he felt I could digest the information, he would give it to me or to others through my trance.

Other Classroom Visitors

During séances, James, as my control entity who decides from the spirit side who is able to speak and who is not, sometimes brings through some spirits who have made their marks in history.

Among these remarkable spirits, Michel de Notredame—Nostradamus—came through several times. Nostradamus was

---

[1] Sophia and Hokmah are the the feminine personification of Wisdom in the Greek and Hebrew traditions, respectively.

born in 1503 and died in 1566. He was a physician who became an astrologer and a prophet. His renown has grown immensely in recent years as we have witnessed the passing of his prognostications. According to my students, Nostradamus never came through for a session. He instead managed to sneak in, saying, "I am Michel de Notredame." This would happen when James was beginning to fade out, and his tone was completely different from James's.

Nostradamus was not the only one who sneaked through. My students have told me that the deceased young actor River Phoenix also came through for brief moments.

I know almost nothing about River Phoenix. I do know that he was an actor. I do not even know when this gentleman died, but I was told he passed from a drug overdose or something similar. He died tragically in the prime of his life. For some reason, he kept visiting us while I was in trance during our séances. James, my control entity, allowed him to come through, so it must mean that in some odd way we share the same soul nucleus. I am so filled with questions and have sought answers to them, but have found that one question leads to so many others that it truly would take an enormous amount of time to follow up on all the new and exciting things on my special journey as a medium. Sometimes I am given a direct and simple answer that completely satisfies my curiosity, but more often this is not the case and I spend hours struggling for one answer to one question. I wish I knew more, but I do not.

Sometimes James would say, "We are bringing in Sir Thomas Hobbes."

Sir Thomas Hobbes was born in Wiltshire, England, in 1588. He was a great British writer on civil disobedience. He wrote *Leviathan*, which advocated his doctrine of sovereignty. Hobbes held that since people are fearful and predatory they must submit to the absolute supremacy of the state, in both secular and religious matters, in order to live by reason and gain lasting preservation. He lived in severe danger of prosecution after the restoration of Charles II. He died in 1679.

It surprised me when I heard Hobbes on the tape speaking with a very heavy British accent. He spoke about how life relates to its environment and the society it grows up in, and how all of us are intertwined. He was very eloquent. He has never come through since I came to Florida in the 1990s.

James was amused because he felt he was learning our native English as spoken by Sir Thomas Hobbes. But Hobbes spoke Old English, and this confused many of us even much more.

Eileen once described in a séance the relationship between James's English and Hobbes's: "He [James] took on several lifetimes and in those lifetimes he remembered the English one, so he is speaking English. And keep in mind, people, he worked so hard to learn your language. He didn't know that modern English *wasn't at all like Old English.* He worked on the words of Shakespeare. He had tried to improve by sounding like he and Thomas Hobbes were one person. He hoped to speak on the Inquisition."

I was very touched that my beloved entity James would take such strides to learn the English language so he could be understood by all of us. Truly, I am humbled by this endearing soul. Thank you, James.

For many years, the spirit of Ernest Miller Hemingway spoke freely through my trance states. The famous American writer had been awarded the Nobel Prize in Literature in 1954 for his mastery of the art of narrative, most recently demonstrated in *The Old Man and the Sea,* and for the influence that he exerted on his contemporary style. He encouraged several of my writer friends to work on their unfinished books. Papa Hemingway also often told writers in our group which pages had to be corrected, which chapters had to be rewritten, how it should be recast, and what syntax should be used. Surprisingly, many listened. Several of them got their books published with the changes he advised and felt obliged to Hemingway. One of the books resulting from Papa's coaching was a fictional book about World War II. Another one was a psychology book whose authors reside in California.

I found it fascinating that certain personalities were allowed to come through, and I once questioned Eileen about this.

She said that the only way that they can come directly into my mind in the same manner as she does is that we all *came from the same soul nucleus.*

She also explained in my trance state to the students, "From Marilyn, Hemingway, Sir Thomas Hobbes, James, Miriam, Shimon, Andrew, to Caesar Aurelius, not Tiberius, we all are part of the same nucleus. I am trying to tell you that there are many of us who come from the same master soul. Each one has to live a mortal life. Sometimes we are on the earth plane together. Sometimes we are not. Until we all have experienced the whole entire spiral of all the lives, we cannot go back to the oneness of the nucleus."

It took me a long time to figure out what she meant.

8

Ten Years with Hemingway

A writer's problem does not change. He himself changes and the world he lives in changes but his problems remain the same. It is always how to write truly and, having found what is true, to project it in such a way that it becomes a part of the experience of the person who reads it.

—Ernest Miller Hemingway (1899–1961)

IN THE EARLY 1970s, other entities began coming through in addition to James. They often communicated with me during my automatic writing. One spirit in particular seemed strong enough to block all others from entering my field of vision or sensing, except, of course, for James, who is always part of all spirit communications that take place. This entity also stayed longer than others. When he came close, I sensed him always as a mature male in his forties or fifties. It was not until several years later that he allowed me to sense him as a young boy.

119

I also sensed his way of talking, which carried a commanding tone, especially when he paused to stress his thoughts. He spoke with power, wisdom, and passion. The man had an incredible way of telling his stories in written form. All of this, I was to learn, came from his experiences that included but were not exclusive to great adventures and sweet loves. He was and still is a giant of a man.

This stranger kept asking me to read Ezra Pound (1885–1972) and E. B. White (1899–1985), the author of *Charlotte's Web*, *Stuart Little*, and *The Trumpet of the Swan*. He also asked me to read books by Sir Arthur Conan Doyle (1859–1930), who wrote not only the Sherlock Holmes stories but also many articles on spiritualism, and by H. G. Wells (1866–1946), who dreamed of a utopian society. I was also introduced to the Fabian Society. Through their eyes, their emotions, and their feelings, I was able to read about the so-called perfect society they wanted to have. Many years later, when I read Eileen Garrett's autobiography (Garrett 2002), I was absolutely shocked and excited to find out that she had read the same work, but she lived it because she was part of the Fabian Society, met Wells, and channeled Conan Doyle in 1931.

Back then, these writers were not those I would normally read, but out of respect for the spirit, I spent lots of time in the library and read whatever I was directed to read. I felt an urgency to finish a book no matter what, even if it was not to my liking or if it was the most boring book in the world. Once I started reading a book, I felt a great need, mostly out of respect for the writer, that it had to be finished. It was my way of honoring the author. Whether living or dead, it does not matter. It was just my feeling and, to a great extent, still is.

As you can imagine, all the writings I was directed to read enhanced my life on many levels. I became so humbled about the work many of these great writers fought hard to get published, sometimes at a great risk to their reputation. What an enormous treat for me to take part in. I was not only reading their works but also feeling their emotions about what they had gone through to write their books. Thus their works directed me to learn more about their lives. Their lives stirred with great passion, and indeed my life took on a greater awareness and meaning.

One day I asked the stranger, "Are you any of these people?"

He said, "Hell no!"

It shocked me to find out that spirits also curse.

Then James instructed me to go to the library. I was walking aimlessly in the aisle of parapsychology books. After a period of time, when it became obvious that nothing was happening, I left that section and began to think maybe I had the message all wrong and should be walking slowly up and down other aisles. So I decided to start with authors whose last names begin with E. To this day I do not know why I started in the E aisle, but perhaps I was directed to do so and did not realize it at the time. While I was slowly going down this E section, out of nowhere and from high above me, a misplaced book titled *For Whom the Bell Tolls* flew off the top shelf and almost hit me on my head. It missed me by a fraction of an inch. I looked around. The E aisle and the neighboring aisle were empty but for me. Then another book rose itself from the shelf. The next book that fell off the shelf was not a threat to my body. This one was titled *The Sun Also Rises*.

I remember thinking the spirits must be having fun with me and that this was some kind of test to see if I could contain myself. I was becoming truly unnerved about what was happening in a very public place filled with people who were very quietly going about their business. I had no choice but to contain myself; after all, there were signs all over saying to be quiet.

While I was holding on to the two books, a physical reaction started to take place in the upper part of my stomach. I felt a slight jumping. My built-in Geiger counter, which is located in my solar plexus, was vibrating and jumping all at the same time. I had broken out in a sweat and was getting very excited. Glancing down at the two books in my hand, I saw the author's name, Ernest Hemingway, in gold letters. I asked myself, "What am I holding these for?" It seemed like a big jolly old man was inside of me, rumbling my stomach and pushing it to laugh. And I felt the laughter heaving up and down. Somewhere in my head I heard, "Swell—job well done!" So I took the books home.

The excitement left me with such an overwhelming need to find answers to the questions buzzing in my thoughts that I could not get any sleep for more than twenty-four hours. At every available moment I sat down and went to my automatic writing, asking, "Is this Ernest Miller Hemingway?"

Asking this question of the spirit over and over was bringing me to the point of exasperation, but I refused to let go. Then with a rush within my body and tingling from head to toe, my Geiger counter began to vibrate. After a few seconds of this physical reaction, my stomach started to rumble in an up-and-down motion. My hands started to shake. Sweat was pouring off of me, yet I was not nervous, only curious and excited as I heard James say, "He is with you. He will teach you." That comment started ten years of growth. Hemingway came in with force and indeed we had quite a shared experience.

The relationship was rocky for the first two years. I labeled him as a misogynist, a manipulator, and a womanizer. I did not like his he-man style. When reading about his personal life, I often felt his emotions, which caused me to feel his desperation along with his heightened excitement. His passions ran deep and when he loved a lady, it was with all his heart. I could not understand how he could hurt these women he married by starting up new relationships with other women. It bothered me greatly how he broke their hearts. So one day I asked him to please allow Hadley and Pauline to speak to me or to take me on a journey so I could meet them. I needed to know they forgave him for his wandering ways.

Imagine the lessons I went through as this gentle giant turned my anger toward him into love and understanding.

What happened was a lovely and pleasant surprise. He did answer my request and allowed me to feel for his wife Hadley. I felt her pain, her suffering, and her heartache, but I also felt her love, joy, and happiness. Although losing Ernest to Pauline hurt her, her love for him was so great that her desire for his happiness seemingly outweighed her heartache over losing him. This did not happen all at once, but in time she became a happy lady again. I found it odd that just about all his conquests shared that same feeling about him. They loved him so much that there was room in their hearts to allow him to be happy with another. That is the essence of some of the discussions of the utopian society H. G. Wells wrote about, where you can love somebody so much that you understand that out of love for the other person, you would allow him or her to get away or be happier, that you would make that happen, even if it is with another man or woman. Hemingway's first wife, Hadley, loved him so much that she was able to do that.

Hemingway was always very good to each wife he divorced. Whatever he had, he made sure that his children and ex-wives were taken care of. And they apparently all became friends. But his ability to maintain a friendship with his exes did not stop me from crying and feeling deep emotional upheaval for every wife. I wept for every wife he cheated on. I used to scream at him, using my strong thoughts in a yelling fashion. I would say, "My guts are being ripped out because I'm feeling your life through these women. How could you do this? You're a mean man. You meanie. You should never get married. You broke all these women's hearts. I can't tolerate you anymore."

I was not of the same mind as Hadley and Pauline were, and I found it very difficult to hide my anger toward Papa, even though his ex-wives accepted him on his terms. Papa would respond by telling me, "Grow up. You're very infantile. Grow up." Looking back at my reaction and his response to my outbursts toward him makes me realize how precious our shared time together truly was. Imagine having this type of conversation with a spirit. What a treasure!

A Budding Relationship

Although very much bothered by Hemingway's chauvinistic and womanizing ways, I gradually became fond of the man. It took a long two years, but my hostile feelings faded away and in their place a fondness grew.

Perhaps it had to do with learning about his life; through him I was able to feel his emotions about the world he lived in as a mortal man. He also invited me to sense his emotions as they related to what was going on in our world during that period of time. Being invited to sense and feel emotions that came from his heart and very core of his spirit was quite incredible and very often left me in tears. As I felt through his emotions, he would also feel mine. Together we touched hearts and amazingly had similar feelings toward many things. He was not afraid of crying or sharing a heartfelt moment. Many times he cried through me as he despaired over mankind destroying our planet by polluting it with toxic waste and how the people in modern times boldly justify their actions by saving it is all in the name of progress. I learned to feel through him on a level that I did not know I was capable of. It was astounding that Papa would open up his heart to me.

A wonderful by-product of having Hemingway with me was that I became less fearful of walking our city streets. Although I knew James took excellent care of me during my time in New York City, Papa added to the feeling and at times I was fearless as I ventured into the so-called bad neighborhoods in New York City. When I ran into somebody with piercing eyes or who appeared threatening, instead of having a "fraidy cat" reaction, I was directed to feel the emotions of what the spirit wanted me to touch in that person. Often I would stare directly into the eyes of that menacing person and words would come out of my mouth that I know I never thought of saying, and it would defuse a possibly harmful situation. It was as if the spirit of Hemingway took over. The city during the 1970s and 1980s was a rough town to navigate through, and because of my daily routine of walking many miles, it was a great comfort to know Papa was adding to my safety.

When Hemingway's spirit came, it often caused me to have a more masculine approach to and view of life, especially as pertains to drinking alcohol. At times, this was unsettling to the spirit of my beloved Chinese medicine lady, June. She made it clear to me she did not like me drinking alcohol, but she understood that Hemingway's desire to taste liquor through me was too great for me to deny. She further added that she would not stay with me during the times I was quenching what she called a "Hemingway thirst." She did just as she said she would, yet somehow I knew she was never far away, and she would indeed come to be with me if needed. I always felt sad if I caused her to leave and was torn over her need to express herself in the manner that she did. In fact, what did happen was that she came into my dreams and continued to take me on her walks in forests where she gathered her herbs and roots. June always has a soothing effect upon my life. I love her dearly.

I could not pull myself away from Hemingway, and the need to explore and learn more was gathering great momentum; thus the saga began.

When Papa was with me on social occasions, all I wanted was Scotch, and I would consume it like it was water. I could have five shots of Scotch in a night. The sixth one would cause me to collapse.

Years later I read A. E. Hotchner's book *Papa Hemingway* (Hotchner 1966). Hotchner wrote that Hemingway once drank a house record of sixteen glasses of daiquiri in one night in a Havana bar called La Florida. The story gave me chills because I couldn't help thinking that I could have become an alcoholic if I had continued to drink Hemingway style, with my body not even feeling the effects of all that booze till the sixth drink touched my lips. Is it any wonder that dear June wanted to be away from me during those times? Somehow I survived Papa's drinking and indeed we were able to move forward in a very positive and informative learning way. My adventure through the feelings of Papa was an incredible road.

Hemingway liked to talk about life and people—their emotional reactions to situations and what they intended to do about the things in life that they were capable of changing. He always challenged me to figure out whether folks were talkers or doers or, in rare cases, both. He stressed his passion for wanting things to be true. He said that writers should tell the truth and write stories as close to the truth as possible, but that sometimes it was OK to bend the truth if it fell into the category of a little benevolent lie. He always said that in order to tell a story, one must live it and experience it; otherwise, one cannot tell the true story.

I have diligently kept a diary every single day of my life. I keep not only a diary for James, but also one for Papa.

On occasion my husband, my daughters, and I would go to Madison Square Garden to watch live wrestling matches. Papa would insist that I take pad and pen because he wanted me to write about what was happening. He refused to allow me to commit anything to memory and said it would be impossible for anyone to capture the events and be truthful about them unless they recorded the major highlights. Wanting to please him, I did as he asked. I wrote down as much as possible and tried hard to capture in writing the exact details. Papa would instruct me to slow down and take time to observe the two men in the arena. He said, "Look at their faces. Try to sense what they are feeling. Learn to understand their work by watching what is happening. And put all this down on paper so we can go over it in detail at another time, and I will teach you how to turn your notes into a good piece of writing. Watch carefully what the man who was flung out of the ring is doing. Is he in real pain? Is his act over? Is he truly disoriented?" He taught me how to go into pause—I was seeing through his questioning of the occurrence. At times he would laugh so hard that my own stomach would rumble. I often felt like I wanted to shout out or tell the "bad guy" to knock it off. I not only got caught up in the moment of the event, but actually felt it through Papa's senses, the exhilaration and his passion for the fun-filled, exciting evening.

It was hard to contain my ladylike manners and to this day, I do not know how I was able to be myself while feeling such surging energy course through my entire body. The interactions that I was privileged to have with Papa were absolutely thrilling and very much alive.

When people asked me, "Why do you take so many notes? You are always writing about something." I would say, "Oh, just to keep a record." I used the excuse that perhaps one day in the far future when my children had kids of their own, they would want to have some written record of what took place and would be overjoyed to share it with their family. I did not tell others that I was also keeping a record for Hemingway. Everything I did with Papa was recorded.

He tried to write through me. He would give me chunks of his thoughts to write. Unfortunately for me and him, when it came to write as one would a book, I could not oblige. I was a terrific note taker and was eager to work for Papa, but I simply could not follow his dialogue and get it down on paper. The endless hours we spent attempting to get one sentence or phrase were more frustrating than ever imagined. He would get annoyed with me and let me know I could never become a writer for him. But I tried, and he continued to move me in that direction, hoping to one day use me to write his unfinished work.

He would tell me to get to writing and stop wasting my time drawing. I used to say, "But I love to draw and I love to write little poems related to each person's life."

He would say, "No, it is childish and it is a waste of time." Then he would laugh, adding, "Besides, you can't draw well." He was not afraid to tell me anything. Please understand that I am a doodler and sometimes I can even draw well. I have been doing this all my life, and as Hemingway has a passion for writing, I too have one for art. My passions are expressed via drawing; his, as a writer and adventurer living a daring life.

I felt inadequate because I was not able to do all that he asked of me.

I desperately gave him as much time as I could to write. I was bad at it, and he had no problem letting me know how frustrated I was making him and that I must feel the same way. He was absolutely correct. I did not know how to listen better so I could get his emotions down on paper as they pertained to whatever event we were writing about. It was hard for me to write about two men slugging it out in an arena and seemingly enjoying the slugfest that left them bruised and in some cases severely harmed. I did not like writing about gore or expressing it in detail. I know I blocked out much of his commentary and for that I am sorry.

While all this was going on, I was still a wife, mom, and homemaker, and studying my other work with James. I could not find time to do work with Hemingway on a regular basis. When we did finally get to it, my poor attitude and dislike of the subject matter he chose greatly interfered with the task at hand. He was not mushy, soft, delicate, or wishy-washy about anything. He made it clear that he came to use me to write and it would be wise for me to learn how to afford him that. I can only imagine how useless he felt I was as a writer for him. The golden verbal material he gave me to write was often so badly written by me that instead of transforming his words and notes, his passion about a subject, into a work of art, it read more like a train wreck. The craft of writing takes great skill and tons of patience. I made no bones about it; I did not know how to write.

When it came down to putting his thoughts on paper, the task was almost like a mental screaming match. I think I frustrated this poor spirit to the point of exasperation, because many times when he moved over my shoulder, I could sense a hissing sound. He knew I was not a writer. He came to me knowing I was open but that I was far from able to feel his feeling to express it on paper the way he would have wanted me to. I was not equipped as a writer to put things into proper form.

I was equally frustrated, and the frustration level I had with Papa was higher than the highest mountain in the world. One day I asked James: "Why would a writer come to a non-writer? Shouldn't a writer go to a writer? A scientist to a scientist? A mathematician to a mathematician?"

James quickly replied, "Well, you don't have any expertise in any of those areas. That makes it that much more challenging and exciting. And the experience becomes a learning lesson for you as well as for Mr. Hemingway."

I couldn't help but think that my lessons had a lot to do with paying attention, patience, and allowing what the spirits must say to me to unfold on their terms, not mine. Nonetheless, I politely agreed to follow up on my interaction with Ernest Miller Hemingway.

Many years later, Eileen told me that James felt that because I was doing so much automatic writing, learning to take chunks of information and put it down on paper would not be a hard thing to do. She added that I had the capacity to comprehend through Hemingway's emotions how to put together the thoughts that were being expressed to me. Regrettably for Papa and me, it did not work out well.

While we were still in the early years of our shared time together, Papa suggested a test and asked me to write a short story for him. This was simply to see if he could relay his thoughts strongly enough to me, and if I could gather them with enough feeling to give me the words. I agreed to this. Although it took many long hours of diligent work on my behalf,

I will forever remember the new set of passions that surged through me. Many a time I felt his emotions and tried desperately to get his words in the proper style down on paper. However, time was precious and simply did not afford me, an extremely busy person, the luxury of losing myself in Papa's world. Once again I did a very poor job. With great difficulty, we managed to finish a short story together. It was called "King Paco & Queen Eve." The dark short story is about a bum who kills a frightened teacher and ultimately pays the price of being killed himself. The story was not only poorly written, but it was written out of what I thought I heard and was being directed to write. Thus the challenge was that after each session of writing down what Papa gave me, I then rewrote it to make it flow in acceptable English language. It became a monstrous task and I shudder thinking back to it.

I sent it out to a major magazine and it was rejected. The editor said it was too short. I was very naive and wrote back, "But it is a short story."

By the time Papa asked me to finish his unfinished work, he was already calling me "Daughter." He even wrote a poem for me, and part of the poem is as follows:

> Come here, come here, little girl, little girl.
> Come sit on my knee today.
> I will watch and hold you and care for you always,
> As we pass the time away.

Parting Ways

About six years into our relationship, I still could not fulfill Hemingway's expectations. One day I said to him half seriously, "Maybe you should seek another writer."

Papa said, "Thank you. I intend to do that—just didn't want to let you down." He then told me that our time was limited and that he had a female writer with whom he would be spending time. She was young, unencumbered with as much work as I was, and was pretty good at writing. Her family understood all about the spirit realm, so she would be freer to work with him. He went on to add that her mother was also a gifted psychic named Rina. Learning our time together was limited, I wrote the following in my journal:

> I'll probably weep a little each day!
> Remembering joys you've cast my way!
> I won't forget the woes that you gave me too!
> I'll remember it all with love
> because I truly loved you.
> It will be hard to forget a spirit such as you—
> I'll love you forever—I will—I do!

Four more years passed, one day he told me he had to leave me to work with a writer who could take down his thoughts. Part of me was elated, but I was also sad. In his teasing manner he said challengingly, "I found somebody younger, more vibrant, and willing to slave for me."

I said, "Good, I am happy. Go."

I wished him luck and told him to be gentle to his new lady friend. Nonetheless, when it was time for him to leave, I was very sad. Papa's departure hurt me. Ten years is a long time to be with a spirit who on a daily basis communicates his deepest thoughts and allows you to share and sense and see life through his eyes. When he first came, it took me two years to accept him into my life, and although we frustrated each other while trying to get his writing done, we shared wonderful things. I got used to his little nuances, his manners, and feeling his thoughts. It felt like I was losing not only a friend, but quite literally part of my being. I had no one to share my sadness with, and it left a giant space within me. I did tell James that I would appreciate it if he never again brought another like Hemingway into my life because it was just too painful to endure the parting. James did not accept my comments and in fact told me I had lots of growing to do and much more learning to do from others in the world of spirits.

Visiting the Hemingway House

In the early 1990s, while visiting Florida, my younger daughter invited me to go with her on a trip to Key West. It was supposed to be an easygoing vacation, and we were to do things that most other tourists did. We visited all the famous nightspots and walked the entire island, having a wonderfully fun time taking in all the sights. To my surprise, my daughter asked if I would like to visit the old Hemingway house. "Wow," I thought, "what an experience this would be." She knew I was reading lots of his stories but at that time had no idea how involved I was with his spirit. I was so thrilled at the prospect of seeing and sensing Papa's way of living. We walked over to the gate of the Ernest Hemingway Home and Museum and looked at a cat with six toes. I thought, "Oh, this must be a descendant of his cats which he always talked about." I was elated to see this animal and felt this was going to be a fantastic sensing day.

As we walked closer to the door of the house, I became extremely nauseous. It seemed like a generator, with a low humming sound in my head, and made my head dizzy and my body nauseous. My body felt like it was spinning at a quick pace. I could barely breathe, and my feet felt like lead. I was almost paralyzed. I knew that if I stepped further into that house, I might lose myself forever. With my head pounding, stomach in high sick mode, and the ground spinning below my feet, I felt that familiar hand touch my shoulder and direct my body, as it has so many other times in the past, toward a safe area away from the house. Once in the safety of the street, where my symptoms slowly faded and I could regain full awareness of myself, free from the grip the Hemingway house held over me, I thanked my beloved James and told him that I truly felt if I were to enter Papa's house, I might have lost myself to that spirit forever. The struggle to be myself was so incredibly hard. Hemingway's house was beckoning me, and I had to fight with every fiber in my being to keep from being overtaken by whatever overpowering force was trying to take over my mind and body.

Continuing to be who I am was more important than surrendering to this enormous hold on me. My life as a wife, mother, and medium for James was my greater want and blessing. I literally felt I would lose my life to Papa in that house. And I did not want to be a Hemingway girl, emotionally, mentally, physically, or spiritually. I made no bones about letting James know that. To this day, I have no desire to challenge what happened that day by going back to Papa's house.

Full Circle

In the late 1990s I met a woman in Florida and gave her a reading. Then she said, "My daughter just finished the unfinished works of Ernest Hemingway. His spirit came to her."

Thus Hemingway began a promising enterprise with my friend's daughter, who lived up north. This was the mother of the writer Hemingway worked with, who is also psychic and does work related to paranormal studies.

At this point, Hemingway had been gone from my life for several years, so meeting Rina brought back good thoughts of what he had to say about her daughter. The fact that they had finished a book together warmed my heart greatly.

I casually said to her, "Really? Does she live in New Jersey?"

"Yes."

"Did she get the book published?"

"No, because they told my daughter it looked like plagiarism. The style was too much like Ernest Hemingway and they refused to publish it."

Reflections on My Time with Papa

I asked James about the ten years I spent with Papa, "Why did you give me that kind of lesson?"

James said, "Marilyn, Hemingway was here to give you a gift. You learned better discipline, value of time, patience, and above all else, what is most important to your life. Remember when you visited Hemingway house? You refused his offer to return to be with him and you were struggling for who and what you were. This was your greatest learning moment as a woman and you set your priorities right there and then. Everyone has to make choices and you made yours then. Hemingway wanted to come back and work with you but I told him his energy and spirit finished what you had to learn and grow from."

I asked if Hemingway was upset with that, and James told me that Hemingway gave me the heartiest laugh and all of heaven rumbled from it. He further added that Hemingway had treated me like a baby compared to others he worked with. Again, thank you, James, for once again keeping me safe on my chosen journey as a wife, mother, and medium.

My mind was racing about all those years spent with Hemingway, wondering why on earth he would consider coming back to someone he knew was incapable of taking down his words correctly. Somehow, I felt better and, although in my gut I know that Papa has peeked in on me from time to time, I feel he does it as a father watching over his daughter and leaves with happiness in knowing that James, Eileen, and June are daily gifting my life.

Hemingway did gift my life. He taught me to go beyond the physical part of seeing a person and to sense the spirit and soul of people. His passion for living everything to its fullest was always an added treat to sense. As a great writer who wrote about adventures he himself lived before turning his work into masterpieces, he was filled with so much compassion for mankind. And I very often felt his anguish for those who were suffering, especially during our long daily walks in the streets of New York City. Together we would meet and greet the homeless and hungry, offering what little I had to spare to them. Although at first I thought he was the cruelest man toward women, a part of me grew to lose my prejudices and arrogance, and it all was slowly replaced with a deep love and deep respect such as one might have toward a father.

As I recall those years, I see that I learned many lessons. I now understand that I should never judge a person until I truly get to know him or her, whether the person is here as mortal or spirit. These words are easily spoken by most of us, but the truth of it is, we all tend to come to conclusions too hastily. Each human being has many facets. Opening up my mind and heart are no longer just empty words. There is much more to a person than what we read about or what we hear about. It is very complicated to truly understand a person, but the lessons I learned from Papa allow me to have greater compassion and understanding. I also feel I am a better teacher in my field. I am careful not to judge hastily and make sure to try to learn all the facts before assessing a problem. It is hard sometimes to know something on a psychic level and separate it from the spiritual level, because I get a double picture. And there are also times when my sensing doesn't come into play, so I must be extra careful not to judge and instead take a wait-and-see approach.

If Hemingway ever comes to me again, I would be most respectful and would hope never to be arrogant toward him. I would certainly not challenge him on the way he treated his ladies. I would disregard that completely and would ask in a teasing manner, "OK, what do we have on the agenda for today and how would you like to express that thought?"

I know Papa is doing a great job teaching other mortals who need him to learn a thing or two about life. My big, white-haired teddy bear is probably laughing loud and causing heaven to rumble much.

Thanks, Papa, for your visit.

9

Diversified Teaching

Every good gift and every perfect gift is from above,
and cometh down from the Father of Light.

—James 1:17

NEW AGE LINGO began to pop up everywhere in the 1980s.
Among some of the terms that were used was one that I needed
to explore and understand better—"channeler." What was this?
Most of all, why can channelers stay fully awake and have
some memory? Is one able to develop this ability in the same
manner as other supersensory abilities? I needed answers to
many questions, and I was determined to find some of them.

Over the course of twelve years, I observed channeling work
at metaphysical chapels, bookstores, lectures, and just about
anywhere I could find it. I was left with mixed feelings. I was
not sure what these people were doing, but I felt certain that
the good ones were definitely connecting and getting messages.
They were able to give messages to those requesting contacts.
They were generally fully awake at all times, although one or
two went into a light altered state of consciousness, and ex-

cellent telepathy happened. The basic differences between my deep-trance work and channeling was that channelers were awake and remembered their sessions, and entities did not use the channeler's mind or present themselves with different personalities. So I inquired of my teachers from the spirit world whether I could learn this well enough to teach it to my students. I feel that some people are born to do mediumistic work and others are not. People might try, but they simply cannot let go of their thoughts enough to have a consistent connection to the spirits.

My spirit teachers laughed at me and said I had been doing channeling in varying degrees all my life. Especially during automatic writing and reading people, I always brought in some spirit entities who shared a life with the person I was talking to, and those entities usually were able to offer something to validate who they were.

This piqued my interest. Did communication by any method to achieve a connection to the spirits mean that channeling was taking place? If so, it may also follow that those gifted psychics who do not label themselves as mediums but who get messages from beyond are also doing channeling work. The curious thing about that is that most psychics I know have a negative feeling toward people who claim to speak with the departed, yet I have often been witness to them doing exactly the same thing as channelers. Perhaps they simply got old-fashioned mediumship work like mine mixed up with what the modern-day channeler does.

Now that I was beginning to understand channeling, the next step was teaching. These classes were called "Altered States of Consciousness." I taught people how to go into a mild dissociative state of mind and explore, in different facets of learning psychic awareness, the diverse ways of connecting to the spirit realm. The courses covered subjects in past-life regression, out-of-body experiences, astral travel, telepathy, psychometry, channeling, table tipping (telekinesis), dowsing, aura healing, self-healing, and so on. These classes turned into wonderful workshops in which students were able to explore and expand their talents to the point of perfecting them in specific areas. Some took to channeling immediately and stayed with it through all their other experiments in psychic awareness. Only a few had the capacity to let go of their consciousness to allow a semi-takeover of their minds and surrender to the spirits to do the type of mediumistic work I do. They were all very good.

I never had a human teacher to guide me through this; everything I learned was given to me by my spirit teacher.

With great care, like a mother watching over her toddler, I gently coaxed, pushed, and successfully helped many of my students bring out their wonderful gifts. The excitement and joy I have experienced watching the blossoming of a medium is beyond measure.

There are several reasons why people come to the type of classes I offer. Among these are a need to satisfy their curiosity, a desire to open up to their natural ability and find a way to use their gifts in their daily lives, and a need to test waters and expand and explore on a more experimental and research level. Very few who attend these classes are nonparticipants. Most folks simply want to learn.

Everyone to date who has come to my classes has continued on a forward path of learning, growing, expanding, and sharing whatever he or she got out of the class. I am very honored to be their teacher and I do know that many who have attended my gatherings came with mixed feelings and narrow thoughts that were slowly replaced with a broadening acceptance and tolerance, allowing themselves to explore and experiment and reach heights they had never thought were possible. Everyone attending sacrificed time. Some had travel difficulties. Some had mates who opposed their joining my groups. Others dealt with a host of other obstacles. Some were challenged with painful disabilities and several who came had only a few short years left to their lives. Those who were willing to put in the time and discipline required to see even the tiniest of rewards stayed to reap greater gains. They came with passions to put to use and were afforded the same in return.

A hearty "thank you" to all my students, who have made and continue to make wonderful magic happen whenever we are together.

Opening the Door

Light meditation with deep-breathing exercises is offered in a typical channeling class because people need to clear away the daily thoughts that clutter their minds. Deep breathing, in my opinion, helps open the mind so it can receive information from the spirits on a deeper psychic level. People interested in practicing the breathing technique can find a breathing and relaxation exercise in appendix A.

I do not allow any type of music during a channeling class because it may interfere with the process and may cause some of my students to conjure rather than opening up to the spirits. When people conjure something, they begin to fantasize and hallucinate. Some even spook themselves, because they have been conditioned by the Hollywood version of what is to take place during a séance. Moreover, what may be soothing to one may be irritating to another.

Nor do I allow the burning of incense or candles. Many people, myself included, are allergic to such items. I also ask that students not use perfumes, colognes, or anything else that could trigger an allergy attack. Basically, anything that might interfere with anyone else in the class is forbidden.

The majority of my students are able to attain a deep and relaxing light altered state of consciousness. Eventually, many learn how to put themselves into a light hypnotic state, and trust me enough to probe and help them through whatever is blocking them from opening up and letting go. Achieving communication between spirit and mortal means affording the entity the highest love, faith, respect, and trust, and putting aside one's own ego. For some, it may also mean that they must let go of fears, superstitions, and the Hollywood version of ghosts and spirits.

Once the door to the spirit realm is opened, there is no turning back. This type of work must never be taken lightly, and certainly those who have the passion to do mediumistic work should consider the challenges that they will face in their personal lives. They must learn to balance their everyday affairs with the flood of information that will continually come into their minds from the spirits. I ask my students to consider what their lives will be like once they make commitment. And I caution them: "When you truly communicate, it does not stop because you are no longer interested in it. In some form or manner it will resurface and become a force in your life."

Past-Life Regression

Many of my students have benefited in their current lives from what they believe to be a past-life regression. Students who choose to follow my instructions are able to regress to a time from a past life and view an event from that existence. I also teach them self-hypnosis so they can do it at their own pace. I never force or tell people that they must do something just because I say so.

I first build up trust and rapport with my students. Then I teach them how to breathe and ask them to slow down the rhythm of their breath. Breathing, as I always point out, is the most important aspect of all the psychic exercises we do. I let the breathing relax their minds and their bodies. Once they are fully relaxed, physically and mentally, I take them on a journey.

I use certain symbols in meditation to bring the students back in time. I want them to know that they are safe. I let them know that they will always come back, and then I tell them to feel comfortable enough to let the calendar slow down to wherever it wants to. I let them choose the time and place that they would like to freeze themselves in.

Stories of Past-Life Regression

The following stories related to past-life regression were collected by Sheree Wu.

Sanda Gane is a student who came to the United States in the late 1970s. Life was hard and food was a big concern. She was always worried that one day her family would not have enough food in the refrigerator. Sanda had become a very successful business owner of a spa chain but still worried about having enough food. She went to grocery stores and bought ten days' worth of food when she did not need it and had no extra storage space in which to keep the food. Then she gave it away.

During one of the past-life regression sessions, she remembered the fear of being without food again. Sanda revealed that she had been a black person in Africa in one lifetime. In that lifetime, she was hungry and tried to steal food. In another regressed lifetime, she was in England, still hungry.

Marilyn told her, "You just have to go back to that lifetime and witness what took place but do not accept the problem into this lifetime."

After several attempts to experience the fear of being hungry from past lives, Sanda was successful in not allowing it to be a part of her current life. Marilyn emphasized to her that she would never be hungry again.

Hearing what Marilyn told her while she was in a deep altered state, Sanda visualized herself writing the word "success" in the sky. She felt that she sent her previous life, with all its hunger issues, back to where it belonged. She added that after a while, her current life changed for the better. It appears that she was able to successfully release her pain. She is now comfortable and free.

ਇੰ ਇੰ ਇੰ

Janet Rosenzweig, another student of Marilyn's, regressed to the mid-1800s. She was a nineteen-year-old gypsy in Hungary. She saw herself ride her horse out of a camp and then meditate near a stone pond. She described her surroundings and what she was wearing.

Although the family of Janet's mother in this lifetime came from Hungary, neither of of her parents spoke Hungarian at all. Janet does not speak Hungarian, either. However, when regressed, Janet said a couple Hungarian words with tears running down her face. After checking with a friend who does speak Hungarian, Janet learned that she was saying the name of her horse was "A Great Horse."

When Marilyn asked her, in her regressed state, where she was in Hungary, Janet said she was in "Budapesh." "Budapest," Marilyn corrected her.

She said, "No, Budapesh."

*We later learned that Budapesh was the correct pronuncia-
tion of the Hungarian city. Budapest is the English name of this
city. Janet said she never knew the word "Budapesh." However, she pronounced the word as Hungarians say it.*

*Janet feels safe and happy to share the experience openly.
Her husband, David, believes that she was really in her past
life in Hungary. She was very emotional when she woke up
and she usually does not act that way.*

Out-of-Body Experience

Many people have out-of-body experiences during their lifetimes. They mostly occur spontaneously during the sleep or
disassociated states, and as a result, people may not even be
aware of those experiences. Individuals can also learn to have
OBEs at will. To do so, people must be totally relaxed and get
rid of the fear that they will never return to their bodies. The
mind will always come back because its home is the body.

My first experiences with astral travel came when I was a
teenager, but it wasn't until much later that I was able to properly appreciate the growth that could come from such experiences. For several years I flew around the skies above New
York City, setting up experiments filled with challenges that
would help me sharpen this ability—and that I could pass on
to my students so that they too could learn and have fun with
astral travel. During many of these out-of-body journeys, I
sensed a man's hand holding firmly onto mine. Sometimes
he placed a hand upon my shoulder. These trips were quite
amazing, and for a long time such travels were a nightly affair.

I knew that it was difficult to harness the occurrence so that
I could direct the destination of the journey. I spent months directing my thoughts to a specific area of the city, or to a friend's
house. When I thought I had achieved success, I contacted the

person whose home I had visited and described in detail things that were in the house and where they were placed, and if possible the layout of the house. I would always choose someone whose home I had never visited.

I always use myself as a guinea pig before offering something to my students, and it was the same with astral travel. Once I learned to properly channel my energy to direct the course of my own journeys, I would start from scratch and present in simple terms to my students what I thought they could accomplish by following a few simple guidelines.

In a typical OBE class, the first task is to bring the mind and body to a quiet and relaxed state. This is achieved by offering a selective type of meditation. As the class is brought through the meditative exercise, there are always a few people who fall asleep. I usually leave them in their chairs and continue to proceed with the rest of the class. As the students go gently into their self-hypnotic state, I plant words of comfort and feeling great in their thoughts. After a while, I suggest they visualize a hot air balloon or other mode of travel that will safely allow them to take a ride upward, away from their physical bodies. During this phase of the exercise, it is important to note that my students have already developed a trust that I will guide them on a safe journey. When I sense they are secure in their envisioned surroundings, I instruct them to enter their balloons or climb onto their magic carpets, or whatever other mode they have chosen, and release anything they see that might be holding their means of travel down. After having them untie their vehicles, I instruct them to slowly enjoy the ride as they rise higher and higher off the ground. Then they are instructed to look down and take notice of how small the people below them look and to see how tiny the trees and houses are getting as they move further up toward the sky. I gently plant in their minds a vision of the sky filled with soft, fluffy white clouds. At this point I ask them to take one last look below and to see how everything is getting smaller and smaller as they continue to go higher and higher.

It is often difficult to tell whether the mind has truly taken its host on an OBE journey. Most people simply look as though they are in a deep sleep, so subtle differences are not easy to discern and I must rely upon students' descriptions to the class of their experience.

When I compare those who have fallen asleep during this exercise to those who feel they traveled, I do see that the travelers have a more relaxed, serene glow around their faces. The travelers never snore or have the spontaneous jerks that sometimes occur in the body while sleeping. Also, each traveler's body appears to be surrounded by a gauzy, off-white cocoon, as if to keep the body safe until the mind returns.

When they come back, they often say to me, "My God, it was like a roaring train in my head. My whole body was tingling. And when I got past the tingling and the roaring sound, I was just flying all over the place without a care in the world. The sensation was incredible and the sights I saw were awesome."

Ninety percent of my students who experienced an OBE felt that it left an indelible impression, and because their experience was good, they wanted to do it again. Even months later, their experience was so powerful and so wonderful that it stayed imprinted upon their minds. Because of the popularity and success of this OBE exercise, I try to offer it as much as possible. To me, this is one of the sweetest things that we are capable of doing. It makes me think about such questions regarding the use of our mind and perhaps the opening up to a wider awareness: If we are truly capable of travel during OBE, what else are our minds capable of doing?

"Astral travel" is the term used to describe one's travels during the OBE. The everlasting imprint this exercise has on many leads me to believe that some of my students are mastering this feat and can easily visit and report back with accuracy where they have traveled. I have tested many students by asking them to visit each other and report back their findings. Every single one who participated in these tests scored over 75 percent. This is incredible. Students visited people they met for the first time in my class and described their apartments or houses. They were able to describe in detail some items and where they were located, including furniture, antiques, and the layout of the house. As I said, once you can control this OBE, you can direct where you want to go.

On a personal note, since I have lived in Florida, I find myself frequently flying over Interstate 95, where I truly have little desire to be, at least on a conscious level. Sometimes I find myself sitting with strangers in their car, and some even seem to sense my presence. Then, the next moment, I am jettisoned into a different vehicle. This makes for very exciting traveling moments. I can report that during my free car rides I always feel at ease and enjoy the moments shared.

One of my favorite places to visit during astral travel is the beach in Palm Beach, Florida. The beach off Worth Avenue is a special place. Often I am pulled to this location and captivated by its beauty. I sit on the sand and stare out at the horizon. My favorite time to visit is just before dawn. Another place I am drawn to is my beloved New York City, where I specifically visit the promenade in Brooklyn Heights, the Metropolitan Museum of Art, and Saint Patrick's Cathedral on Fifth Avenue.

Whenever I am determined to do mind travel and am able to focus on where I want to visit, I am usually rewarded with what I ask for. Like everything else I do, however, it requires practice; if I do not use this ability for a long period of time, I must practice my exercises so I can become better at it. But the ability to use astral travel as a way to visit the places one loves is wonderful, and I encourage my students to practice at it so they can learn and share and grow from their own beautiful out-of-body experiences.

Spontaneous Occurrences

When an individual is opening up his or her mind, body, heart, spirit, and soul to prepare psychologically, mentally, physically, emotionally to allow a connection to take place, he or she must understand that many of these occurrences happen spontaneously. When people try to replicate the event, they often will find they cannot do so.

I teach my students to maintain good discipline and strong faith. They need to tell themselves, "I've reached this point of my existence, where I am accepting that life continues in a different form that has intelligence. It is the intelligence that I choose to be part of and to learn and to grow from and with." This way if a spontaneous occurrence should happen while one is working at developing these skills, the occurrence will be seen as a wonderful extra event, but one will have the knowledge to achieve communication through other means.

Communication can come in many forms. Verbal communication is only one facet. Others have it via dreaming, writing, singing, drawing, dancing, and so on, and feel very strongly about where their material is coming from. I have also heard many healers say that they truly believe that their power comes from those in the spirit world. Some say the ability comes from God.

Learning how to harness and control your interaction with the spirits is what is at stake. The more you practice, the better you will get. Just like any other skills in life, in order for the magic of this skill to blossom, it requires determination, discipline, patience, and devotion. In other words, richer experience will render clearer communication with those who have passed.

This is hard, serious work, and not everyone has the inclination or the time to do it. Nor should they think it can be part of their lives on a part-time basis. Those who are pretending will eventually get bored with this and fall by the wayside. As James said, one must have faith. This process takes many months, and, for some, years.

Requesting Clarity

Regarding the clarity of spiritual communication, Eileen once said, "Demand clarity of us and you will receive it better."

I asked, "Just that?"

"That's all you ever have to do. Ask." Thus she brought everything to a simple state.

I understand that I am only a tool. I am only as good as what I am getting, whether it is received in my mind's eye as a picture or via spoken communication. I always hope and pray in the course of the conversation that what I am receiving is clear enough for me to successfully convey the messages to the person I am reading. Based on what I was taught by the spirits, I require my students to practice in a well-lit room and encourage them to seek the simplest and most direct approach when they are learning to succeed at communication. I tell them in a simple and direct fashion to ask the spirits for clarity. Clarity is the most important thing to ask for. It reduces the risk of getting muddled information and then having to pore over what was said. One must ask for clarity over and over in one's mind before opening up to a channeling or trance session.

If the students always ask for clarity, the spirits respect them. They begin to understand that by doing this they will achieve a higher level of communication with the spirit world. My students are not going to say, "Hey, give me the best shot." Instead, they may say, "I am ready to receive and I ask for clarity." If their thoughts are jumbled and they confuse the spirits with their lack of clarity, then they are going to get mumbo jumbo in return. This is no different from questioning a teacher or somebody that you respect about an answer that lacks clarity.

People must demand clarity in all areas of this work, including their dreams. Students must keep impeccable notes and be thoroughly honest about what takes place. They need to keep a pad and pen near their beds so they can write down whatever they can recall upon awakening. After a few months, the puzzle will fit together and reveal some information.

Trance Mediums

Finally, we saw the emergence of channelers, and I am very proud to have played a small role in their development. Some students go on to become the best psychics in town. Others become fine platform channelers. Some become excellent healers. Some become a little bit of everything. Out of thousands of students, I have come across nine other physical mediums who have the ability to do trance work. Out of the nine, six disciplined themselves to finally be able to let go of their fear or enough of their control so they were comfortable in doing trance work. Their rewards were slow in coming, but are everlasting, especially the mediumistic ability.

I can teach channeling to anyone, but a trance medium has to be born with that ability. I have never come across a trance medium who asked to do this work; it appears that spirits seek trance mediums out. Little by little, trance mediums open up to the awareness that they are given. The trance mediums I know had similar experiences to mine at very young ages. Likewise, at some point in their lives they felt the need to address what was happening to them. Trance mediums have little control over their bodies and no memory of what takes place during a trance, whereas most channelers remember everything and their bodies are not affected. I believe that those who do deep-trance work need only to understand what is happening and to have a helping hand on their journey, but they do not need a teacher. On the other hand, channelers work on a high intuitive level that tunes into the spirit world. Whether learned as a skill or coming to them from the spirits, communication is taking place.

My student JK is believed to be channeling Daniel Dunglas Home (1833–1886). D. D. Home was described as "the most celebrated medium of all time." When JK first came to me, I looked at this quiet, conservative, young senior gentleman who had fought in World War II and stood guard at the Nuremberg trials. I said, "I don't have to tell you this, but you are a medium."

JK said, "I am a *what*?"

I said, "Take it easy, my friend. It turns out you've got a man in spirit next to you who is telling me his name is Daniel Home."

He asked, "Who is Daniel Home?"

I said, "I don't have the vaguest idea, but we must investigate this after class when we have time to do research about him."

We went to the library to find out Home's identity, and we also asked Eileen, "Who is this Daniel Home?"

Eileen said, "Oh, Marilyn, he was one of the greatest mediums. I used to admire him. I once went to where he lived in England and stood under his windows to feel his essence."

I said, "It turns out that my student will soon be channeling him."

Eileen asked, "Who do you think gave you that information?"

I replied, "Oh! You did?"

She said, "Yes, I did. He doesn't have to work with him, but DDH requested that he keep his promise and open up to him. JK is a medium."

Although the tempo of JK's channeling of Home was slow, he did gradually open up his capacity and make himself available for Home to speak through his voice.

Table Tipping

Besides the classes I mentioned above, table tipping was also very popular. It demonstrates our ability of psychokinesis, or mind over matter. I cannot say if spirit hands are involved or if it is because of high energy put into a table, but movement comes and sometimes we do get gentle taps.

I used to teach table tipping at midnight at Su Casa, a hotel located in the outskirts of Woodstock, New York. Its owners would teasingly say to me, "Marilyn, let the table go crazy. Let it crash through my window. What we will do is cement it in and it will become an attraction."

I said, "No, no. I don't want to be responsible for that. Thank you."

Before beginning a class, I first made sure the lights were on and the room was bright. I then asked for four to six big round oak tables. Each table was six to nine feet in diameter and had steel rods at the bottom. The tables were so sturdy that there was little chance that people could move them. I wanted something so solid that they would say, "Oh my God! This is my energy that is going to move this giant sturdy table."

Then I asked a group of people to sit around a table. Sometimes as many as fifty people would come to the room just to watch this event. Sometimes only nine or ten people out of fifty would join in the actual exercise of moving tables. The others preferred to watch. I asked those who watched to do the mantra with us so that their energies were given to us, too. Usually I asked people to go dancing in the lounge before entering the room so when they came back to me, their energy was high. The magic always happened and people patiently listened and participated, following my instructions.

After every participant touched the table, I brought them into a light meditation filled with the suggestion that they were able to do this and to imagine that the table was as light as a feather. Then they became relaxed and their state of mind was filled with focused high energy.

I made certain commands, asking them to do a mantra, saying something like, "Move table, move table, move table, move!" It sounded like a song. We kept reciting it for ten to twenty minutes.

The table would start grumbling. We felt tingling in our fingers, as if the top of the table was rippling. We felt the energy going down from our bodies into the table. I directed participants' attention to not let go and to allow the table to move and put their energy into it.

If spirits were near and they wanted to help, we would let them participate, too. In other words, I brought all connected energy into the task.

Then the tables usually began to shimmy, rocking a little bit from side to side. A table started to tip over a little, then it reached a balance point and just hung there without moving. Then the tables started to slowly turn round and round and round until they were going so fast that all the people around each table needed to run with it. We once put a French girl on top of a table, and it still spun around and around and around, in spite of the weight.

Then I asked the participants to take their hands off after they had successfully tipped the table. They became excited when they realized that the table still had their energy in it and it moved a little bit.

Then everyone put their hands on the table and asked it to calm down.

One time a man came to me, saying, "I'm a physicist, and I sat down here with the group to prove you're a fraud. But sitting there with the people, there is no way anybody could have done what I think I just witnessed." He added, "Nobody could have reached the pedestal of the bottom of the table with their foot. Nobody let go of it. Everybody was sitting perfectly still."

This same man had admonished his wife for partaking in this exercise the night before. After he examined the tables that were used for table tipping, or, in some instances, table dancing, he told me that the steel rods encased in the middle of the table were impossible for human hands to twist in the configuration they were left in as a result of our activities. Thus he went on to add that he needed to further explore the whys and hows of it all, but admitted it was fascinating at the very least and he was duly impressed. He also apologized to me and his wife.

He added, "It really happens."

10

Ghost Phenomena

One short sleep past, we wake eternally,
And death shall be no more.

—John Donne (1572–1631)

LIVING IN BROOKLYN Heights was like having a daily love affair with New York City. The neighborhood in which I lived was distinguished as a historic district. Each street is filled with the history of past events. Some of these streets have beautiful old carriage houses that have been converted into apartments, while most of the Heights has the original brownstones, proudly displaying the year in which they were built. Some date back to the eighteenth and nineteenth centuries. One can walk down any street and feel the powerful energy emanating from these old buildings. Brooklyn Heights is one of those magical places in America where ghosts are very prevalent, and these spirits from yesteryear feel very comfortable walking around and making themselves known.

Ghostly manifestations presented themselves on many occasions. They usually dressed in the garb of their era. Certain streets seemed to have more activity than others. Ghosts regularly took a stroll or entered these majestic buildings. Being able to witness these spirits was a special treat. I believe that almost everyone, at least one time during their stay in my neighborhood, sensed and felt them, even if they refuse to admit it. Perhaps they might say to themselves, "Oh, this is Brooklyn Heights. What else would you expect here?"

Many of my friends were also sensitive to the uniqueness of Brooklyn Heights. Some admitted they thought they saw a ghost or two. But in those days, this topic was still something one did not discuss openly.

My angelic spirit friends loved this neighborhood, too. They would direct my feet down a certain street just in time for me to see ghosts, fashionably dressed for their afternoon stroll. Some female ghosts wore hats with large satin bows in addition to elegant dresses with fan-front bodice; capped, close-fitting long sleeves; and elegantly pleated, three-tier flounced skirts. These must have come from the Victorian era. Others seemed to be dressed from the 1920s flapper period and wore bobbed hair, fringed skirts, and bold scarves.

I do not know if these ghosts were aware of my presence, because most of the time they simply went about their business and ignored me. It seems that ghosts just want to do what they have always being doing.

Hotel Workers

We had a little cottage in upstate New York where we spent our summers—to get away from the hustle and bustle of city noise, pollution, and crowds, and enjoy the serenity that country living offers. Our house sat atop a hill that abutted the entrance to a forest. When one entered this forest, the man-made paths led to several locations. One of these paths led to a big hotel.

People often cut through the forest as a shortcut to the hotel. I used to see young men in white shirts and dark pants walking up toward the forest to where the hotel was.

One day while I sat outside reading a book, two men dressed in their work attire walked toward me. They looked very normal and I was about to say hello—except they continued to walk past me and right through the walls of my house. This was during the day, with the sun shining bright and other people going about their daily routine. I remember thinking my neighbors were unaware of the phenomenon that was taking place and I was honored to be witness to this event.

I smiled to myself as I observed these manifestations. They were just going about doing what they usually did in their lifetimes—taking a shortcut through the forest to get to the hotel. Their faces were expressionless. To me, their actions were very benign. Someone else seeing something like that may have panicked and made a fairy tale out of it, but I would not do that. They were simply doing what was normal for them.

There are people who passed over who seemingly are locked in the ghost manifestation. In my opinion, that is where they want to be. Just like the ghosts in Brooklyn Heights go about their daily rituals, many ghosts elsewhere are doing the same because it is where they want to be. For whatever reason they have the need to continue, and I also believe that it has something to do with where they must be.

My friendly ghosts in upstate New York would come and go as they pleased. They never tried to communicate with me. After a while I lost interest in studying them.

My Neighborhood

When my neighbor down the hall passed away, I kept seeing him in his ghostly form trying to open the lock on his door.

One day while I was waiting for the elevator, I saw him again fussing over his locked door. I said, "Hi, Allie. How are you?"

He turned around and looked at me.

Then I said mentally to him, "You don't have to try to unlock it. You can walk right in. Just think about being in the apartment and you are there."

After I said this to him, I never again saw him trying to unlock his front door.

Poltergeist in Our Apartment

When my husband and I were first married, we lived in an apartment in the Clinton Hill section of Brooklyn. Being used to seeing ghosts throughout my youth and adulthood allowed me surety that they truly are interested in whatever time period they are locked in. So my first encounter with poltergeist activity was a new thing to learn and surprisingly, I was frightened by it. What took place in my next-door neighbor's apartment in 1965 was significantly different. At first I thought it was just a lady weeping, but when the sound turned into wailing accompanied by loud knocks, it became apparent to me that something dreadful might be occurring.

Whatever was in the adjacent apartment spilled over into mine. The lights in my bedroom and foyer dimmed. It got icy cold in certain spots, yet my body was perspiring. And the prevalent sound was akin to someone screeching chalk across a blackboard. This became unbearable, and I was not accustomed to such poor manners.

I do not like rude behavior, whether from ghost or mortal, so I stood my ground and mentally yelled at the noisemaker to stop. I thought it had ceased the activity and I went back to my bedroom to retire for the evening. As I entered my room, the door slammed shut behind me and loud laughter could be heard throughout my apartment. I tried to open my door but found it was locked and could not be budged. Because I did not want to agitate this ghost further, I slipped under the covers and attempted to go to sleep. Around 3 AM, I awakened to the banging noise of my bedroom door opening and closing. The poltergeist was not finished with me.

Instead of being calm, I got very angry and yelled out loud for it to stop. I said it would please me much if we could have a conversation. The answer I got back came in the form of an awful odor: the smell of rotten fish filled the room.

I said nothing more and asked for spirit intervention from my angelic force. I do not know what was done, but whatever action they took made the poltergeist leave, taking the stench of rotten fish with it.

The next day I asked my neighbor if she had heard any noise the previous night. I will never forget the look of fright that came across this lady's face. She asked if we could have a private chat and made me promise not to discuss anything she spoke of with her husband or any other neighbor. Little did she realize that I was a champion at keeping secrets.

She told me about her endless nights of sleeplessness during which she heard a woman wailing and knocking on doors. She heard children crying and begging for help. And she told me about a smell that gagged her. I stayed silent until she was finished then shared what had happened in my apartment the previous night. I did not want to tell her about my lifelong personal involvement with the spirit world, so I simply said: "Please be aware: whenever this sort of thing should happen again, feel free to speak with me at any hour, day or night."

The disturbances continued for several more days and then stopped. A few months later, my neighbor and her husband moved out of state.

Afterward, I spent time probing. In my local library I was able to read the history of my neighborhood to learn whether there had been any unusual deaths. I was looking for suicides and murders. Some of the information I found was written specifically about the building in which I lived.

There were several deaths that piqued my curiosity. Among them were two children who either jumped or were forced to jump out of their seventh-floor window. Upon further investigation it was revealed that they were twins, and both had Down syndrome. Their mother, who was raising them alone, was cleared of any wrongdoing. I asked another neighbor about this, and she told me it was not uncommon for people in our building to see and hear those children. She herself witnessed them walking through her living room. They had jumped from the apartment above hers. I told her about my visit and asked about the lady who wails. She surmised it was their mother, who had recently passed away.

This was not an easy discussion for us to have, but my neighbor was eager to talk. She was thankful to bring it out in the open. Further chats with her proved to be invaluable, specifically those relating to the other three suicides that had happened in our building.

The noisy ghosts did not bother me very much, but many of my neighbors said they were frightened by the activity that went on each year on the anniversary of the deaths of the twins. When we shared our stories, we were amazed at the similarities.

A New Next-Door Neighbor

The apartment next door did not stay vacant for long. The new tenants were a young family just like ours. Over the course of three years we became very friendly. The activity emanating from that apartment started again about a year after they moved in. The wife was unaware of the previous events, and I preferred to keep it quiet because she was easily spooked. Nevertheless, she called me in one day and asked me to look in her bedroom. I saw what appeared to be a human form sleeping under the blanket. She concurred that this was exactly what she had seen. I knew her husband was at work and did not want to add to her stress, since she had to stay in the apartment alone with her child. With her permission, I quietly approached the bed and said, "Whoever is lying in the bed, please go elsewhere."

The ghost of a man rose up and left. My neighbor was somewhat shaken by this ordeal and divulged further that her privacy had been violated over the course of the past few days. The occurrences had all the earmarks of the return of poltergeist activity. She told me of her typewriter typing by itself and of hearing weeping and seeing the shadows of what she thought were children. It got so bad that even the babysitters she hired would not return because they heard voices and saw things move by unseen forces.

I witnessed an old Underwood typewriter hit the space bar and type the letter *X* over and over across a page. The activity stayed within her apartment, never once coming back into mine. The ghosts never harmed anyone, but they seemed intent on getting our attention. My neighbor was in a frightful state. As soon as her husband found a job elsewhere, they moved.

Have a Cup of Tea

A few years later, a friend who also resided in the building called to tell me of her strange experiences with ghosts. Hearing the slight edge of fear in her voice, I tried hard to lighten it up by telling her to set a table for them and invite them for tea. She took my advice seriously and called to thank me, saying after that, "they never returned."

Looking back, it saddens me to know that although many people are willing to accept the appearance of a ghost, they refuse the possibility of communicating with them. Fear, superstition, and ignorance cause people to miss great opportunities to talk with those entities with whom we share space. My experiences have led me to believe that ghosts can elevate to a level where they can communicate if they so choose, and it is up to us to try to offer a chat with them.

Back in my Brooklyn Heights apartment, I helped another friend to communicate with a ghost. She lived on the seventeenth floor and I lived on the twentieth floor. Her daughter's bedroom was three floors below my older daughter's bedroom.

When my older daughter was still very young, I woke up one night to hear a noise emanating from her bedroom. Upon entering her room, I did not smell anything, but I saw a dark shadow. The shadow was hovering over my child in an attempt to fix her cover. And I thought, "Uh-oh, we've got a ghost."

I mentally said, "Come with me. Come with me. Get away from my daughter. Come with me." I walked out to my living room and sat down on the couch. Then I mentally said, "Be my guest. Sit down." The ghost listened, sat opposite me for about twenty seconds, and then disappeared through the floor.

The next morning, I got a call from my friend asking for help. She was unaware of what had happened in my apartment and how I asked the ghost to leave my daughter alone. She told me that she had seen a ghost in her daughter's bedroom the night before. She went on to say that she wet herself from the fright of the ordeal. I asked her why she chose to share this with me, and she said she felt I was the only person who would understand and not make fun of her. She meant her comments in a normal fashion: Since our daughters had the same bedroom three floors apart, it seemed logical to her to forewarn me, and based upon our personal conversations, which covered many subjects, she knew I was very understanding. At that time she was not aware of my ability. I believe this particular friend, with whom I was not that close, was working on an intuitive level although she was completely unaware of it at that time.

I said, "You're not going to believe this, but that same ghost was in my daughter's room and was hovering over her bed."

She said, "Please come downstairs and please help me."

I said, "Well, I think that ghost lives in our building. I think it's one of the old ladies who passed."

I went downstairs. I waited for the ghost and I said, "Please come back."

Eventually I invited the ghost to come back upstairs. I said, "Please, I'd appreciate if you do not hang around my two daughters. It would be my pleasure to have you as guest. Come shopping with me. We can have fun together. You can go to school with me. You can help me teach children how to read in school when I volunteer to do remedial reading. We can do a host of things together."

I never heard another word from my friend about this ghost returning to her daughter's bedroom. She even went out of her way to avoid the discussion. Quite frankly, at that time, I was glad that it ended quietly. I could see where some of my friends would be frightened because they did not understand. People tend to translate that kind of occurrence into a more complex thing than it really is. Most people have so much *fear* of ghosts, conditioned by what is pumped into their heads by Hollywood.

All most people ever have to do when they run into a ghost is to say, "Please leave." If that doesn't work, my beloved Eileen says, "Invite us for a cup of tea." Many people I have met think that in order to have the company of a spirit, or to get rid of the spirit, they must go through some kind of ritualistic procedure to please the spirits, often resulting in nonsense. Eileen has told me often enough that these rituals amuse the spirit realm and that literally legions of them go to rituals to watch the ridiculous ways we behave. I suppose the spirit realm has fun laughing at us mortals doing the silliest of things. Perhaps Eileen's suggestion of offering ghosts and spirits a cup of tea is a way of saying "Welcome to my house"—and it helps to eliminate *fear*—although many people I have known who have experienced ghostly manifestations would faint from the experience if a ghost decided to take them up on the offer.

I feel blessed that I am not afraid. When I run into the ghost, I have the same attitude I had in my youth. When I perform an exorcism, I always tell ghost or spirit: "Hey, come on, come share my table with me. Let's have a chat. It is OK if you can't talk or I don't understand your thoughts because we're not connecting. Let's give it some time and I promise you we will get through this."

Even though I know the ghosts don't drink, I am always very courteous and offer them tea or coffee. I invite them to stay, ask them if they have a message, and always try to make them feel welcome. I tell them that I understand that in their ghost form they can't give me a message, but perhaps they can speak with my spirit friends, James and Eileen, who will help them to communicate with me or guide them to a better level of understanding so they can get rid of anything that might be troubling them.

Ghosts manifest themselves in their human forms. In other

words, if a ghost lived as a mortal in 1890, it may choose to come back from that lifetime, with the dress and everything else from that time period.

As for spirits in non-ghost form, I have found them to be much more sophisticated and intelligent. They are free to choose a period of time from any lifetimes they have lived and want to share with us. Spirits can do things many ghosts that haunt one particular area can't, including, if they want to, pulling away and manifesting themselves as ghosts so we can see what they looked like as mortals in the lifetime they choose to show. This is usually done so we can have a visual of them, but this ghostly form is brief. They enjoy speaking to us directly by entering our thoughts or helping us develop other forms of communication.

Poltergeists make their presence known for a reason. I always want to know their reasons, to see how I can help bring resolution and closure.

Funerals

My friend Doris and I once attended a memorial service in one of the oldest and most beautiful churches in Brooklyn Heights. As the speakers were giving their heartfelt speeches about the dearly departed, I saw the essence of a ghost begin to emerge. At first it was very light in appearance, but as each speech was given and words of adoration filled the church, the ghostly manifestation became clearer.

After the service, we were invited to the family's home to continue to pay our respects. Doris and I chose a small couch to sit on. I sat down first, and I noticed that the ghost sat down next to me, leaving little room for my friend to sit.

I was getting uncomfortable, worrying about two things: first, telling Doris she would sit on the deceased if she continued to move closer to me, and second, knowing that my friend might easily be frightened when she learned.

I decided to take a direct approach and told her she was sitting inches from the ghost and she had best move over to give him more space on the couch. Doris was cool about this. She not only moved over but said loudly, "Marilyn, I must leave. Would you please come with me?"

A few weeks later we learned that other people who attended the funeral service for our neighbor were sharing their stories about seeing him walk in the hallway of our building.

At another funeral for a dear friend who died suddenly from a fast-moving brain tumor, several of my students and I gathered in a church to say good-bye.

Sitting atop her casket and smiling out at all of us was Desi. She made a point of letting us know she was very much alive and was enjoying herself as she listened to what the priest was saying. After the service, every one of my students reported seeing Desi on top of her casket. In an odd way, it brought us comfort.

Perhaps these ghosts and spirits are letting those of us with sight know that they do not want to be remembered lying at rest in a casket or an urn. Maybe they show up at their funerals to make this point clear. During my numerous séances, one of the first things many spirits ask their surviving family is, "I'm always in the house. Why do you keep coming to the cemetery? I hate that place."

When I tell this to people, they are very often shocked because the only place they feel they can find solace is in the cemetery where they laid their beloved to rest. However odd this may seem to many—and I do appreciate it is contrary to what most people think—a lot of spirits and ghosts really do not want to be in a cemetery. They all say they find solace just being around their families and watching their lives continue. They do not like somber feelings. They don't like to be near us when we are sad, remorseful, angry, or feeling any other emotions that they feel stunt our growth.

Since spirits love to have fun and ask me to take them places that bring laughter to each day, I often tease them by saying: "I am walking through the wall. I am walking through the wall. Can you see the wall? I am walking through the wall."

They respond in kind, telling me, "That lesson was already learned when you were a child. Should you proceed to attempt such an act, you will wind up with a major body bruise."

On our daily walks, we look for funny things to lighten the hurts we feel from the people we meet on the street. Among such things are humorous signs that have double meanings, or children at play laughing loudly, dogs running off leash and playing in a park, or even watching the birds at play. Of course, we have serious times together, too, as when they are teaching me how to open up to another facet in paranormal studies.

From what I have witnessed and learned over many years of attending funerals and going to cemeteries, it is clear that ghosts and spirits want to continue in their existence away from where they are interred.

An Exorcism in Sheepshead Bay

When people suspect that they have poltergeist activity in their house, I recommend that they first go through all the logical steps that one would normally take to find out why these noises are occurring. There are many possible causes for noises in a home; having a poltergeist is a rare one among them.

For instance, an electric current running under the house

can cause chaos and noise, and it can also affect the magnetic flow underneath the house, which can affect the electricity, water, and so on. A door that does not close right also makes noises. Your house may be sloping very gently so that regardless of what you do to keep a door closed, it simply wouldn't happen. When a person tells me that a faucet goes on in a house by itself, I ask that person to check the plumbing and make sure it is in good working order, and to pay attention to the handles on the faucets and adjust them if they are not tight enough. The temperature of the water coming out from the faucets may be the result of the water heater being adjusted incorrectly.

If a person still feels uncomfortable after eliminating all other possible causes, then it may be time to speak to someone like me. And if he or she is not hallucinating, exaggerating, or lying, I will certainly offer whatever assistance possible.

I am not a psychologist. I have no way of judging whether a person is fantasizing or not. So I have to depend on my psychic feeling and senses. Most important is the trust toward my beloved spirits, James and Eileen, who guide me through the task of an exorcism should one be required.

Among my last jobs in New York City in the early 1990s was to help a young mother who called me in desperation. She believed her apartment, which was located in the Sheepshead Bay section of Brooklyn, was being haunted by a poltergeist. She was fearful and concerned about her young daughter's life.

Whenever I work as an exorcist, I demand that the host follow my rules. Only family members are allowed to be present. No media, including reporters from TV, radio, and newspapers, should be contacted. The host cannot light candles, incense, or anything else that would permeate the building with smells.

I always bring a few people who are not squeamish about the occurrences to offer help by competently recording the event, and two or three other psychics who can offer their impressions. When possible, I include someone from the medical field, just in case someone faints due to fright.

The host at the Sheepshead Bay did not listen to my requirements. When we arrived at her home, we were greeted by more than twenty people. She apologized, explaining that she had told one friend and the news got out of hand. Before long, more of her friends demanded to come. Her house was packed.

This was not a good beginning for the work ahead of me. Yet, determined to help this woman and her daughter, I simply told them what might happen and asked them to follow my instructions. Then I placed them into several different groups. One group stayed downstairs and the other three groups were placed in different upstairs rooms—the mother's bedroom, the daughter's bedroom, and the bathroom.

There was a thickness in the air. It blanketed the entire second floor of the house, and was thicker in the child's room than in the rest of the floor. A hamster in its cage appeared to be spinning upside down.

Before I began asking questions of the spirit, I needed to check up on all my teams. I asked my group to stay put in the child's bedroom and told them that I would return shortly.

I first checked on the group I had asked to stay in the upstairs bathroom. I knocked on the door several times, but the group did not acknowledge me. Instead, I heard loud laughter coming from inside and was annoyed that these people were not responding. I tried to open the door, but it was locked. So I ran downstairs and went out into the yard. Looking up at the bathroom window, I could see that the light was on and heard loud laughter coming from that room.

I returned to the bathroom door and continued to knock on it. Then the door suddenly flung open. Angry at these people, I was ready to ask them to leave. But they were at a loss when they saw me. They told me that the door had closed and locked behind them. They had no light to see by because it would not go on. I told them what I had seen and heard. None of them had heard my knocks at the door. They claimed to have felt cold hands touch their heads. These darlings were freaked out. This one little incident scared them enough to leave the upstairs and stay put down on the first floor.

We continued to explore and concluded that the girl's bedroom was the most active spot in the house. I had a hunch that the spirit wanted a male to work through, so it was important to have a volunteer to back up this mission. I told the team that we needed a male volunteer. One man was eager to volunteer, but he was not the one our spirit friend had in mind. It became apparent that the spirit had selected another man, whose name was Peter. Peter suddenly sat on the floor of the girl's bedroom with a very spacey look upon his face, while the rest of his body went limp.

Peter started to gently weep. Then the weeping turned into hard sobbing. At that point, James put me into a trance. James then spoke to Peter and put Peter into a state of mind where he was able to tell us that the ghost of a little boy was near. Peter channeled the little boy. We discovered that the little boy had died as a result of a fall when he slipped off the rear fire escape and hit his head on the concrete. His father had been a known alcoholic who often beat his wife and son. According to the ghost, his father had been wrongly accused of his death. Then the father came through and told us that what his son said was the truth.

There were actually two ghosts in that house, but it was the little boy that caused all the problems. James then reported that the little boy had come into the room and the father and son were able to be reunited. Peter broke out crying. He cried like a baby. James then asked the boy to leave the family that he was haunting and blend into the soul that had borne him.

Having finished the work, we left. I feel it is up to the people we leave behind to investigate and verify the information that is given to them. The host checked the history of the house and confirmed that a little boy had indeed accidentally fallen down the fire escape. Because the father was abusive, the neighbors thought that he had pushed the boy down and accused him wrongly. The father was charged with murder.

The funny side to this once serious and fearful situation was that I got a call from the mother a week later. She asked, "Could you bring the ghost of the little boy back? My daughter misses him."

Haunted Church in Florida

In the mid-1990s, after I moved to Florida, many parishioners of a nearby church complained about being bothered while sitting in the church. Women felt their ankles being scratched, and very offensive smells and loud noises interrupted the sermon. The situation became so serious that the number of parishioners coming to the church dwindled down to almost nothing. The deacon of the church discreetly invited several people from various religious denominations to perform an exorcism. Their work did not achieve the goal. Other mediums who were called upon refused to enter the church because they claimed that evil lurked within its walls.

Finally I was contacted. I took my usual group—several other psychics, another medium, and the people who invited us to rid their church of poltergeist activity. We had tape recorders and cameras, and someone to document everything that was said.

When I arrived at the church, my solar plexus started to jump. This physical reaction usually indicates something is about to happen. Perspiration was pouring out of me, and I felt dizzy and nauseous. Yet I instinctively knew this was not a house of evil but simply had a spirit who was very angry about something. I went to the altar and was told by James to lie down on the floor and he would do the rest.

Through my trance, James communicated with the spirit that was wreaking havoc upon the parishioners. He spoke in what might have been ancient Aramaic and Latin. The spirit told James why he was so angry: He was a former pastor of the church, and he was furious with the new pastor, who fooled around with women. The spirit showed his disdain by causing bad smells and scratching the legs of the female parishioners. After James talked with the spirit, he was able to restore calm to a turbulent situation.

Before I left, as is my usual habit, I rechecked everything to make sure our job was successful. As I reopened the doors to the church, I was given a signal by the spirit that all was well. Behind the altar was a giant stained glass window. It lit up for me. No lights were on, and sun did not cast a light through it. The faint aroma of myrrh lingered. I knew that my angelic force, led by James, had performed a little miracle on that day.

As far as I know, the church replaced the pastor and has been free of its spirit troubles for many years.

Coco and Blossom

Most of the time people do not know that they can have fun with ghosts. My student and friend Rita Rudow is an exception.

In Florida in the early 1990s, I met a woman named Judy, who asked if I would help her get rid of an annoying spirit that liked to move things around in her house. Judy said the activity from the unseen ghost frightened her.

Rita went with me to Judy's house. I went into a full-trance state and James spoke. James made contact with the imps causing the trouble and reported that two little sisters, Coco and Blossom, used to live in the house where Judy now lived. They had been murdered in the 1930s. They thought it was funny to scare Judy.

The ghosts agreed to leave, but James believed that they needed some nurturing. He asked Rita if she could take care of Coco and Blossom; he would deliver them to her house. Rita is a retired New York City elementary school teacher who understands the psyche of children. She felt privileged that James thought enough of her to suggest she take on this task. Besides, Rita thought it would be amusing to watch things move and hear the ghosts' laughter. So it was a perfect arrangement.

Thus, Coco and Blossom lived in Rita's house, where plush stuffed animals, ceramic doll angels in beautiful attire, and hundreds of unicorns in varying sizes were abundant. They stayed on one of the beds in her bedroom. She called them "ghosties." She would go into the bedroom, feel the cold spots, and say, "I know you are here. I hope you like it. Now you have toys." She would greet them in the mornings and at night. Occasionally Rita would come home and find the plush toys on the floor. She would verbally chastise them and say, "Blossom and Coco, while you live with me, kindly do not mess up my house."

From that moment, the toys stayed on the bed and the pictures were not turned. They behaved themselves.

A year later, James told Rita that Coco and Blossom had

been in her house long enough. They had their experience and it was time for them to move on. Rita had always understood that when James was ready, he would take them elsewhere. Still, she felt sad when that day came.

Ghosts in My Class

For many years I taught different levels of psychic development classes in an apartment in the Bay Ridge section of Brooklyn. This particular apartment was haunted by ghosts. The apartment that our host had previously lived in was also very much haunted, and had the honor of being mentioned in a book as one of the most haunted places in America. It also was investigated by a prestigious New York City psychic research center.

On occasion, ghosts would become active and we were all able to see, hear, smell, and sense their presence. Items would be rearranged or disappear. Ghostly faces would watch us from various parts of the house. Sometimes they would stare at us from outside a living-room window, which was curious because the apartment was located on the third floor. Unseen hands would touch us, usually around the face and head. Some of the women who attended were squeamish, while the men showed only poker faces.

One night I asked the class to be prepared for a lesson in dowsing. After I explained what to do and put them through several exercises, we decided to take our dowsing rods out into the hallway. In the exercises, several of the men in our group were blindfolded with rods in hand. While they were doing this, a young couple coming back from a date climbed the stairs to return to their own apartment. One gentleman's rod started to twitch toward the couple. Coinciding with this scene was a strange noise that can only be described as an eerie "oohhh" and "aahhh" emanating from our host's apartment.

Our group was intent on completing the exercise and, accustomed to the ghosts pulling pranks, we simply ignored their noises. Not so for the unfortunate couple. With ashen white faces, they fled the building as if their lives had depended on the precipitate action.

I received a call the next day from the host, Linda. She told me the young couple was very scared. They were terrified to return to the building, and the girl's father had to forcibly push her past my friend's apartment. We made sure to never again bring our work out into the hallway, but we continued to hold several more years of classes in her home. Ghosts always attended and were an active part of our evening.

After I moved to Florida, the ghost phenomena continued. On occasion they visit my classes. These gentle beings have been known to superimpose their essence upon several of my students during classes. We always accept them. We realize that not everyone would invite ghosts and spirits to a class, but we do not have this rule.

My groups focus on making contact, and we will and have extended our love to include those from the spirit realm. Regardless of how they want to make their presence known to us, they are all welcomed. To me they are a force of love and they come with light. The spirits or ghosts always encourage us to celebrate our existence while casually empowering us all to enhance our awareness. They offer us rainbows filled with rays of hope.

Very few of my students are of a squeamish nature about seeing ghosts and experiencing spirit communication. It is understood that it may occur, and when it does, it seems to have a wonderful effect on the students. For some, it helps validate what they always hoped was true—that life continues after the mortal body dies. Communication from these heavenly bodies, especially James, seems to clinch the belief for most. My angelic team puts everyone at ease and my students feel as if they are having a natural chat with their best friends.

11

Animals and Plants

But Solomon talked to a butterfly,
As a man would talk to a man.
                    —Rudyard Kipling (1865–1936)

IT IS INTERESTING to learn that animals can manifest as spirits, too. My own experiences make me wonder if all species are capable of doing this. I usually do not listen to plants or animals unless I am within their proximity and there is something they want to say. If their message is important, it will be communicated. My encounters with animals, mortal or spirit, are so hilarious that sometimes I feel that I am like Dr. Dolittle.[1]

My Dog Snooky

When I was a kid, I fussed for days, begging my parents to allow me to have a dog. We were poor, and my father wouldn't

---

[1] Dr. Dolittle is a fictious character in Hugh Lofting's classic children's tales and a few movies based on the tales. Dr. Dolittle is a doctor for people but later on becomes one for animals thanks to his unusual gift of the ability to talk to animals.

let me get a big dog, fearing it would be too costly to feed. So, as a compromise to my pleas, he said OK to a small one. My mother made it clear that the animal would be my responsibility to walk and feed and clean up after should it make a mess. I agreed to everything and pretty much did as promised, except when I was ill and required bed rest.

My mother and I went to a dog pound. We saw this little dog looking at us, and I knew she would be mine. As we tried to look at other puppies in the adjacent cage, my dog rushed to the front of hers and kept barking for my attention. The cage was opened and the next thing I knew, she jumped right into my open arms.

We named her Snooky. Snooky was a fox terrier/beagle mix. She had the coloring of a fox terrier but the face and short hair of a beagle. We quickly became pals and were inseparable: We ate, played, and slept together, spending every minute I wasn't in school joined at the hip. She was the joy of my life.

Snooky lived for eleven years. After she died, I felt her jump up on my bed, just like she used to when she would cuddle her head next to mine on my pillow. One night both my mother and I heard her lapping up water from her bowl. Another time we heard her fingernails on our old linoleum floor, making a "pita-patter-pita-patter" sound. And every time it rained I smelled that unmistakable aroma of wet dog fur. Her spirit stayed with us until we moved from that apartment several years later.

Many years later, my husband and I were driving through my old neighborhood, looking at the changes. My building was no longer there. The old tenement, a condemned World War II–era building that should have been demolished before I was born, had been torn down to make way for more modern affordable housing.

As we approached the spot where my building used to be, I saw a little dog with the same markings and colors as my Snooky walking in my direction. I had to keep my emotions in check and my mouth closed because my husband didn't know much about me being able to see ghosts. I mentally grabbed Snooky to my heart and sent her silent messages and visions of me stroking her and giving her endless hugs and kisses. I also sent her a strong message asking her to come with me now and live with me forever. My beloved ghost dog must have heard me because she turned to look at me before fading away. This was a memorable day and I felt a beautiful gift was given to me.

Since that episode, the spirit of Snooky has come to visit and stayed for a few days at a time. Whenever that happens, I mentally tell her to come to sleep with me. I always feel the sensation of her licking my face during her visits. It is beautiful—just beautiful.

When Snooky was alive, she was my confidante and comrade when I saw the ghosts of people. She would bark nonstop and often tried to chase them through walls. I laugh now at her doing this, because I used to try to do the same. Thank you, Snooky, for being my dog. I love you forever.

My Cat Lucifer

My family and I had a special relationship with my cat. His real name was Lucifer because he was jet black, but I called him Lu-e or LuLu, mainly because it did not seem polite to call out his full name in the presence of other people.

When I got my Lu-e, he was only a month old. He was too young to be pulled away from his own mother, but the child who was giving away the kittens had to get rid of them.

He was a beautiful little black kitten, but I worried that my husband might not accept him. I told that cat, "You have to convince my husband that you are welcome in the house."

We took him home, made a bed for him from an old tissue box, and bought little toys for him to play with. After making him comfortable and letting him know how much we loved him, we left him on his own for about an hour. While my husband was taking a nap, this little kitten managed to get out of his tissue box and climb up to where my husband was napping. He then proceeded to empty his tiny bladder on my husband's back. We did not know whether to laugh or cry—my husband was angry, but the situation was hilarious. In private my daughters and I howled with laughter, and we three agreed this was indeed a very special cat.

Lu-e and I were like one mind. We lived on the twentieth floor and I was afraid that he would fall off the terrace. I would mentally tell him, "Don't go too close to the edge. Be a good boy." He listened to me.

It took me a long time to trust him enough to allow him to wander free on our property in upstate New York. He would disappear for hours and I was concerned that he would fall prey to other animals. My husband had a healthier attitude, insisting that Lu-e be free to romp and play and roam wherever he chose to go. Several times my concern peaked when, after I called his name loudly, he didn't respond. But many hours later he would show up at our doorstep and meow to be let in. His daily treks through the forest unnerved me, and, like a mother worrying where her child is, my emotions ran deep with the same concern. It took a while for me to remember that I could put my abilities into action to call him. With practice and determination, I was successful. Often I would get a message back from him telling me he was OK, just lying in the sun near an old oak tree. I did not depend solely on this ability to mentally communicate with him, but through most of his life it was something the two of us shared. On a special level, we were able to get into each other's minds.

Lu-e developed feline leukemia when he was eighteen years old. He had always been a thin cat, but his weight dropped to three and a half pounds. The doctor suggested we put him to sleep because he was in a lot of pain.

I asked James, "Is this his time to die?" He said, "No."

I said to the doctor, "I will take my cat home. I will see if I can nurture him back to health."

The doctor said, "Marilyn, you could never do that. You will accomplish nothing and will be prolonging his suffering."

I took this little, skinny, dying cat home and told my daughters, "For however long it takes I will be devoting every moment to keeping Lu-e with me, and this includes while cooking, cleaning, and all other chores that need my attention."

At this point in his illness he could not empty his bladder, and most of his vital functions were barely working. He was far from healthy, but when my James said it was not his time to die and that with care I could bring him back to health, I refused to put him down. My belief in what I was told gave me a strong faith, and I needed to make him better.

Each day I wrapped him in a soft cloth and tied it to my body so he could feel the warmth of my flesh and hear my heartbeat. Sometimes I felt his tiny bones give a slight wiggle against my bosom. I fed him milk with a doll's bottle and then massaged his tummy in hopes of making it work. I opened up vitamin E and fish oil gel pills and squirted them into his mouth. He had not eaten solids for more than two weeks, but he allowed me to feed him the milk and vitamins. He wiggled more and more often, and finally he was nurtured back to life. My daughters were extremely supportive of me throughout this ordeal. We filled Lu-e's head with thoughts of love and never left him alone for a second. He lived until he was almost twenty-three years old.

In 1987, when my father was dying, my cat once again did not look good. I said to him, "I am saying good-bye for the last time. I know that you will not be here when I return." I was crying and very heavy hearted, but I had to see my father, who was on his deathbed in South Carolina. During my plane ride, I mentally talked to my father, sending him visions of old movies he loved and telling him, "Hold on, Dad. I am coming. I am coming. Make sure you stay alive until I get there." My nephew picked me up at the airport and told me my dad was babbling nonsense about old movies and to tell me to hurry up and get to him. This confirmed that sending visions to him had worked, and he was indeed waiting for me to say good-bye. I got there and spoke to him. After a while he asked me to leave so he could travel home. He said he needed to be alone. We both knew we would never see each other again. He died shortly after I left the hospital.

That evening I received a phone call from my daughter. She said, "Mom, we are in the animal hospital. Lu has to die now. He can't make it without you here."

I was ripped to pieces. The hospital was kind enough to put the telephone to the cat's ear. I was able to talk to him as his eyes were closing and he went to sleep forever.

My younger daughter, Jane, was so brave. She held him until he died. At that point, even if I had been there, he could not have been nurtured back to health. James told me his time was over, and I believed him. Lu-e and my father died on the same day. I felt I had lost both my son and dad.

After Lu-e died, I tried to conjure him for days and days. I saw him in my mind jumping on the furniture, playing string games with me as he used to do, or sitting next to me on the stove top while I was writing in my diary. But it wasn't real.

Several weeks passed, and I held fast to a vision of Lu-e in his healthy, happy state as a mortal cat. One day while writing in my diary, I saw a thin black tail out of the corner of my eye. Then the rest of the body slowly emerged into a full-sized black cat. My Lu-e was in ghost form, doing what he always loved to do—perch atop our gas range and feel the warmth from the pilot lights while I wrote in my diary.

I was looking at him, and he looked back at me. As I reached to pick him up and cuddle him in my arms, his ghost disappeared. I did not conjure or have wishful thinking going on. My cat truly came for a visit. Since that time he has visited me on many occasions, but he never stays long.

Thank you, Lu. We love you so much.

Sadie

In 1992, while I was visiting New York City, my girlfriend and I were browsing in a bookstore when I heard my name being called. I paid no attention. My name was called again. The voice said, "Marilyn, come to the back of the store. This is Sadie."

I walked to the rear and saw a lady sitting there by herself. I looked at her and assumed she called me. I said, "Excuse me, did you call my name?"

She said, "No."

I told her, "It was a woman's voice and the voice said her name was Sadie. Is there anyone here with that name?"

Then she said, "Maybe it was the cat." She pointed to a little black cat sitting on the floor that was staring into my eyes.

I do not usually hear what animals say, except for the telepathy I shared with my cat Lu-e. I can pick up on some of their thoughts and have done some telepathy with them, but I haven't really applied my work to sense more and certainly never heard one call me by name.

The cat was speaking to me, somehow connecting to my thoughts. I found myself mentally talking back, saying, "Thank you for calling me." I told her that she was beautiful and that her name was very special to my life. She answered by saying she knew this and that was one reason she asked to meet me.

I left the shop but did not get too far because halfway down the street, I had this nagging feeling I should return. The more I tried to ignore it, the worse it became. So we returned to the store and I hurriedly went to the back looking for the lady who had introduced me to Sadie. She was nowhere to be found.

I asked the clerk in front of the store where she and Sadie were. He asked me to describe her and the cat. He told me the lady had passed away a few months ago, and that she used to sit in the rear of the store talking to Sadie. He went on to say that the cat was still around, and he was pleased that his friend had made contact and thanked me for sharing the event with him. I was touched deeply by this remarkable cat and her ghost friend. Their visit will forever be a memorable one.

Sam and Miss Piggy

In the mid-1990s, I got a call from a lady who had a sick horse. She asked me if I could please come to her farm and offer some help or possibly do a healing on her horse.

I said, "I have a friend who does terrific healings." I was referring to Rita Rudow, who has a pair of golden hands.

When Rita and I visited the farm, we saw the biggest horse that either of us had ever seen in our lives. Rita was intimidated by this frisky, nipping, neighing horse. The horse was so huge that when Rita stood near it, the top of her head just barely reached its chest, and Rita looked tiny by comparison.

While Rita patiently attempted to heal the horse, I took a walk around the farm. Ten minutes later, I heard my name being called. I turned around but I did not see anyone. Then again I heard a man's voice in my head, "Marilyn, come back to the stable."

I went back to the stable and looked for the man who was calling me. All I saw was Rita, who was still afraid to touch that giant beast, and our host. I went over to our host and asked, "Did you call me? Or was there a man around here who stepped outside to call me? I was way out in the field."

She said, "No."

I said, "OK. Do you mind if I sit here?" And with that, I heard in my head again, "Wow, it's about time you came here."

I looked at the horse, and the horse looked at me. He said, "I want to tell you a story. Please tell it to my owner."

I replied mentally, "OK, I am all ears."

"Tell her to please not put me to pasture. I don't want to go up to Virginia. I like it down here in Florida. Tell her that I have two more good years to run. And I am sorry that I knocked down the stall next to me, but she put this beautiful filly next to me and I really want to make love. And my name is Sam, not Mike."

I delivered the message to the owner. She said, "Oh my God. I have everything set up to move him in a few weeks. I was going to sign the papers to send him to Virginia. You realize that based on what you are telling me, I am not going to send him away now, because what he told you is true. Two days ago he broke down the stall to get to the female horse next to him. We thought he was getting crazy."

I continued to tell her what her horse was saying to me. "She should have known that I want that filly. That was why

I broke down the stall." Then he said in a soft British voice, "I have finished speaking to you, Marilyn. Now I will allow your friend to touch me."

I asked, "What did you say?" He said, "You can tell the healer that she has my permission to touch me now."

Then I looked at Rita and said, "Rita, he is ready for you. He won't hurt you. Go ahead and touch him." Finally, Rita was able to put her hands on him and gave him a nice healing.

As we approached the car, I said, "Oh, wait a minute. I hear Suzie calling out to me."

I asked the owner, "Who is Suzie?"

She replied that Suzie was her potbellied pig. From early childhood I had a special fondness for pigs. I ran all the way back to the stables to meet Suzie.

There she was, the most beautiful little fat black potbellied pig, walking toward me. I said, "Hello." She looked at me and said softly, "So you are Marilyn, who just spoke to Sam?"

I said, "Yes, and I sense you hurting too. Do you want me to bring the healer back? Rita is her name."

Suzie said to me, "No. I've got a spur on the bottom of my thigh. Could you please take it off?"

I said, "No, I don't want to touch you. I don't want to hurt you."

She replied, "I know. I know. Tell the owner. She will bend down and unplug it."

I looked at the owner and told her what a perfect ending to this day was, and I felt so fortunate to be a part of it and so very honored to have spoken with her animals, but the greatest gift of the day was speaking with Miss Suzie. Then I added, "She is telling me she has something stuck on her thigh. She would appreciate it if you could take it off. She thinks it is a spur. She said it is very hard for her to walk around with this because it is causing an irritation."

When the owner looked down at this little pig's thigh, she was amazed to see that the spur was indeed where the pig said it was. She pulled off the spur. Now it was time for me to leave. I said thank you to this Miss Piggy and to Sam, who apparently dismissed me after his conversation was done.

Once again all the dogs were lined up in a row, as if to salute Rita for her healings and me for having communicated with them. Rita was feeling happy because she had helped them. I was feeling happy for Rita because she helped Sam. My elation was over Miss Piggy, which was the gift of the day, and both Rita and I left flying high, knowing it was a job well done. We both knew some wonderful magic had taken place, each with our own abilities to help and share with the animals. We felt very blessed.

Big Bertha

Plants are alive and sensitive. We may not communicate on the same level, but they certainly can feel our emotions.

I used to have more than two hundred plants in my apartment in New York City, many of which I had started myself from seeds and cuttings. I loved to watch them grow. I talked to my plants and told them how much I loved them and how beautiful they were.

When I cut a limb of a tree or an overflowing hedge, I always say to the plant first, "I am sorry. I have to give you a hair cut. I would like to let you grow wild, but the neighbors would complain. I apologize for hurting you." I do the talking. They do the listening. I don't know if it helps.

When plants are vibrant, I can sense them. I believe everyone can. When you go to a plant store, you may notice that some plants are so perky that they want to talk to you. When you pass by a plant, take a look at it and say, "Gee, you are beautiful." You may feel the leaves move toward you as if they were appreciating your compliment.

One day in the late 1990s, when I was leaving my friend Sharon McConnell's house, I said, "Sharon, there is a female by the name of Bertha. Bertha is saying that she needs water. She is thirsty." Sharon looked at me and said, "Say that name again." I said, "Bertha. She is thirsty. Maybe she is coming from the spirit world. I don't know. But whoever this Bertha is, she is very thirsty."

Sharon laughed and said, "Marilyn, turn around." I turned around, but I didn't see anything but a bunch of trees.

She said, "Look in front of you. Do you see a giant slash pine tree?"

I said, "Yeah."

She said, "Look at the Philodendron[2] that wraps herself around the pine tree. The plant was given to me when it was a baby, and it grew so quickly that we named her Big Bertha. She needs a lot of water."

---

[2]This plant is native to tropical American rain forests. Its name is from the Greek *phileo*, meaning "to love," and *dendron*, meaning "tree," referring to its love for climbing trees. Also known as *Elephant Ears*.

12

Boundless Love

Sheree Wu

> *Her body sleeps in Capel's monument,*
> *And her immortal part with angels lives.*
> —Romeo and Juliet, Act V. Sc. 1

Chatting with My Father

After our very first phone call, during which Marilyn delivered the messages from my father, I decided to arrange a family session with Marilyn over a three-way call with my mother in my house in the Silicon Valley and my older brother, Charles, in Tallahassee, Florida. My mother and my brother were skeptical about spirit communication. Even though they did not express their doubts in front of me, I could feel their skepticism. I knew that they agreed to participate only because they did not want to hurt my feelings.

I was aggrieved, but I did not confront them directly. Instead, I felt that I could appeal directly to my father for aid. I

191

decided to approach this by asking after his mother.

ða ða ða

My paternal grandmother died in northern China in the mid-1930s, when my father was nine years old. At that time, the whole family was on the road, running from the Japanese invasion. Before they were able to properly bury my grandmother, the Japanese troops came. The rest of the family had to immediately flee, leaving the coffin behind. When they returned, my grandmother's body had disappeared.

This unsolved mystery created indelible pain for my father. In 1999 he was taken suddenly ill with leukemia in Taiwan. One day my eldest cousin, Hsiao-Chin, went to the hospital to visit my father, who was feeble and, following the recommendation of his doctors, rarely talked to visitors. But that day, my father made an effort to say to my cousin, "Hsiao-Chin, you have got to find your grandmother."

My cousin answered, "Uncle, you will get well soon. Once you recover, we will go to China together to find Grandmother."

Hearing this, my father sighed like a tire being flattened.

I knew my cousin was only trying to cheer up my father. Meanwhile, we all knew my father's unfinished task of finding his mother's body would remain unaccomplished. It saddened me to think that my father's final wish was not fulfilled and he passed away in the grip of such frustration.

Thus, with my father's unfinished task in mind, before the phone session with Marilyn on March 27, 2003, I mentally pleaded with my father twice a day for two weeks: "Dad, if it is really you who will come through, please kindly let me know if Grandma is with you. How is Grandma? Is she all right? I won't ask Marilyn. Instead, you have to announce it yourself. Please let me hear it. Please, Dad. This is a secret between you and me."

` In the meantime, I deliberately avoided mentioning anything about my family to Marilyn before the scheduled session because I did not want to feed her information or otherwise prepare her. In fact, contrary to what many people might guess, Marilyn herself also stresses that if her clients divulge any personal information, the reading will be contaminated. She does not want to be told anything, and she does not want to see any pictures, either.

⋆ ⋆ ⋆

On the appointed day when Marilyn answered the phone, the first thing she said was, "Sheree, we've got your father here. He wants me to tell you that he is with your Nei1-Nei? She is all right."

At that moment, I knew that my beloved father heard my plea and he was telling me that he was with Nai3-Nai (奶奶), which means paternal grandmother in Chinese.

Then Marilyn said to my mother, "Su, your husband feels bad that he didn't have more for you."

My mother sobbed when she heard this. My father had been a high-ranking government official in Taiwan. From our early childhood, we children were taught by my father that we should reject all the gifts or red envelopes from people who came to lobby or make a connection. If we accidentally accepted those gifts or red envelopes, upon returning home and learning about them, my father would take whoever accepted them to the gift sender's home to return them.

In order to bring more income to the family, my mother held two teaching jobs. I am sure the acknowledgement of this meant more to my mother than anything she'd ever been told. She kept sobbing and weeping.

Marilyn continued saying, "Your husband wasn't the easiest man in the world, but he thinks he was. At least with

Sheree he was. Is it true?"

Both Charles and I agreed: "Yes."

"He was harder on the boys. Is that true?"

My brother smiled. "Yes."

"Sometimes he was harder on your mother. Correct?"

My mother suddenly interjected, "I don't think so."

Marilyn sighed fondly, and continued, "He is saying that he was not an easy man. He is saying that he was a good man, but not as easy as he could have been. He says that he mostly wants the respect and admiration of his children. And he wound up teaching his children, too."

Then Marilyn continued, "He is showing me a road with pebbles on it. Black and white stones on this road. He is saying that his space in heaven is beautiful."

Marilyn then asked my mother, "Su, are you aware how much your husband loves you?"

My mother did not answer, so I answered for her, "Yes, my mother understands."

Marilyn said, "And do you know that his love is never ending? He still has that much respect and deep love for her. And he apologizes for any time he ever made her life hard. To his beautiful wife, he wants all of you to make sure to check out her stomach and her health. She has been straining herself. Su, have you been taking care of yourself?"

My mother said, "Yes."

Marilyn asked, "Have you been going to the doctor?"

My mother said, "Yes."

Marilyn asked, "Is your blood pressure very low?"

"Yes."

Marilyn said, "Your husband says he doesn't like it that low. He says you are not eating properly. Is it true?"

My mother said, "I just do not eat very much."

Marilyn said, "He knows that. He is very concerned about that. He says it's your way of beating yourself up. He doesn't understand why his beautiful wife would do that. He says, 'Honor me by making yourself healthy.' OK?"

My mother said, "Yes, I will."

"He says, 'You have given me breath and joy every day.' You understand that?"

My mother answered, "Yes."

Marilyn went on, "He says, 'Please do not miss me because I am always near you.' He says yesterday he tried to sit with you in your favorite chair. You didn't realize it and you pushed him away. You think he is a fly. He is laughing. Su, he wants you to laugh again.

"By the way, did you know he was loyal to you for all the time you were together?"

My mother said, "Yes."

Marilyn then said, "And did you know that he knew that you were loyal to him, too?"

My mother said, "I think so."

Marilyn said, "He thanks you for that. He feels sad that you refuse to find romance. But he is happy that he was so good that you won't allow another."

Hearing these messages, my mother, still depressed about my father's passing, clutched my hand and cried.

⁚ ⁚ ⁚

My mother is the only daughter of a general who forever lost favor from Chiang Kai-shek in 1949. In 1960, despite her parents' disapproval, my mother ran away from the family to marry my father, a man without much money or power. Faced with such unprecedented rebellion, my grandmother thought her daughter neither respected her authority nor appreciated her intention that my mother could marry well and live an affluent life. As a result, my grandmother was enraged and immediately renounced her daughter.

My father had lost his own mother at a young age, and he did not want my mother to suffer from a similar misfortune. He asked various people to exhort my mother's parents, especially my grandmother, to forgive and reconcile with her. Five years after my parents married, and one month after I was born, my grandmother finally permitted them to return home. On that day, in front of my grandparents' neighbors and friends, my parents knelt down and bowed all the way from the entrance of the village to my grandparents' door, so that my grandmother felt that she earned her face back.

Whenever I think of this story, I feel the depth of my father's love and kindness toward my mother. He loved her so much that he was willing to sacrifice his own dignity to rebuild the relationship between my mother and her mother. Indeed, my father and my mother were considered a model couple among their friends, and their enduring love is still envied by many. My father's passing in 1999 was such a deep loss that my mother barely talked to anyone or left the house afterward. My brothers and I were worried, but we did not know how to help her. My mother did not listen when we told her to eat well; she did not listen when we told her to take a walk. She rejected all of our suggestions.

While my mother was in anguish over my father's death, the only topic she could engage herself in was my father. Nothing else mattered to her.

One day in 2001 my mother suddenly said to me, "We should have appealed for the help from traditional Chinese medicine. Perhaps the Chinese doctors might have had some way to save your father."

I did not know what to say to her, but I felt that I needed to say something to console her. I said, "Mom, please don't think much now. Perhaps Dad now is very happy since he finally does not have to suffer from the pain."

My mother immediately said, "He is happy? We poor surviving ones are not happy—we miss him."

I found that my remarks could not comfort her, so I said, "Mom, think this way—you and Dad were married for thirty-nine years. It was already a long time to be together by fate."

I thought I was smart enough to pull my mother out of her misery, but my mother retorted, "Thirty-nine years? Forty-nine years, fifty-nine years, ninety-nine years—I still want to be married to him."

Hearing these words, I could not come up with any more words of comfort. In fact, like many of their traditional Chinese peers, my parents never mentioned the word "love" in public, or even in front of us children. Therefore, these words are my mother's confession of her whole life, and they carry the same weight as a pouring rain after a drought.

❦ ❦ ❦

I told my brothers about the conversation I'd had with our mother, and we still did not know how to help her reconstruct her life. However, during the family session, Marilyn addressed our concerns for our mother without any hint from us. She said, "Your husband says, 'Su, you don't have to be so fussy anymore. You can relax in the house. You don't have to make everything perfect anymore.' Su, your husband wants you to walk and take care of yourself. He wants you to walk at least a mile a day when the weather is good and feel the fresh air. He says, 'Don't hurry up home; it's not the time for you to go home yet. Honor me by making yourself healthy. Please do not miss me because I'm always near you.' "

During the conversation, Marilyn asked my mother, "Did your husband smoke a lot long time ago?"

My mother said, "No. Never."

Marilyn then said, "His father? Somebody, another man there near him is smoking with him."

My mother said, "I see; my father-in-law. My husband once told me that his father was a chain smoker."

My brother and I were astounded because we did not know that our grandfather smoked at all. We never knew him or even saw a picture of him. "Grandpa" was just a vague term for us. Our father came to Taiwan as a refugee student following the retreating government. For many years my father hoped he could see his father alive some day. Then in the 1990s he finally learned his father had passed away in China during the Cultural Revolution in the late 1960s.

Marilyn said to Charles, "Your father says he is near your family very, very often, too. He has learned how to fragment himself, which means he can be with all of you at the same time. For that matter, did your children tell you they thought they saw or heard him?"

My brother was not certain, but later we found out that his son Jason once said that he saw my father after he passed away.

Marilyn said, "He wouldn't want you to get upset about that, if that happens. He wouldn't stick around that way. He would try to enter your thoughts, not to come in a physical form because he wouldn't want to frighten anyone. The only one he would come physically to would be his wife because she would understand. Su would know, if she saw him, it wouldn't be in her mind. He would actually try to manifest himself."

Marilyn then said, "Now your father says, 'Tell them I love the goat.' Who's the goat?"

All three of us laughed, "Jenni, Charles's daughter. She is the only goat in our family."[1]

⁂

Since my younger brother's first son was born after my father passed away, my mother was curious about whether my father had a message for this child. She asked Marilyn, "Did my husband mention about the first child of Richard, my second son?"

Marilyn replied: "The one who died?"

My mother said, "No." She thought Marilyn did not understand her question. Then she added, "No, the first child of my son Richard."

Charles and I suddenly understood what Marilyn meant and yielded, "The second."

My brother Richard's wife, Anita, had indeed had a miscarriage before her son Justin was born. From Marilyn's point of view, the miscarried child was the first child of my younger brother. So Marilyn was correct about the miscarriage.

Marilyn continued, "No, he is only asking about the name. He emphasizes tradition. I don't understand what it means."

As for tradition in picking a name, we knew what it meant.

When my father was in the hospital, Charles and I tried to lighten up my father's mood and asked, "Dad, our younger brother is going to have a baby. Would you like to pick a Chinese name for the baby?"

My father, who had picked the Chinese names for Charles's children, said tiredly, "Whatever your younger brother feels like is fine."

Three months after my father's passing, little Justin was born. Richard picked Jing-Heng (敬恆) as Justin's Chinese

---

[1] Jenni was born in the year of goat.

name. The first character of Justin's Chinese given name is Jing (敬). It was predetermined by our family tree. In the Wu family, every person of Justin's generation will have Jing, meaning "respect," as the first character of the given name, just like every one of my generation has Hsiao (孝), meaning "filial," as the first character of the given name. This is what our father meant by tradition. A person's name tells which generation he or she belongs to.

After delivering my father's messages specifically to each of us, Marilyn said, "April. April. April. April brings showers, my family—Sheree, is there a ceremony in the family soon? Your father is saying he is going to this. He is showing me the cemeteries. And your father keeps saying 'celebration.'"

I realized what my father meant. Qing-Ming Festival (清明節) was coming the following month. It is a tradition that Chinese worship at the ancestors' graves on that day. I had already arranged to take my mother to sweep my father's tomb on that day.

"Yes, Marilyn, we understand what that means. Well, we have not associated this word, 'celebration,' with this day."

"Your father is saying the word 'celebration.' Actually it is not uncommon. 'Celebration of life' is the phrase many spirits use when referring to funerals or memorials. Your father also says, 'Bring the red flowers.' He says that's the Chinese symbol for good luck?"

"Yes, indeed. Red color is a symbol for good luck."

"He is going to this. Is it OK with you?"

"Of course."

"He doesn't want to see anybody crying. He wants to see everybody happy."

Marilyn continued, "Su, your husband is asking that you buy the special cookie. Please taste one so that he can taste it through your mouth. He likes to feel it through you because you are his wife and he can feel through you. He says, 'We don't need food obviously, but our memories of food linger.'"

At the end of our session, Charles said, "Marilyn, I have one last question. Does my father know we really miss him very much?"

"That you miss him?" she repeated. "Yes. Not only that, he also knows that you had sweaty palms before you got on the phone tonight."

I heard my brother chuckle at his end while Marilyn continued, "He also knows that your neck bothers you sometimes, but you don't tell that to the rest of the family. He also knows that you had an injury on one of your arms."

"Yes." My brother said the word in a significantly lower volume.

"He was near you. He wants you to know that. He says you are a very brilliant young man. He is so proud of you that a father couldn't be more proud of a son if he tried. He thanks you for your loyalty and your love. He says make sure to get your mouth checked—you have a dental appointment to keep."

"That's right." My brother again spoke with a hard-to-hear volume.

"Correct?" Marilyn asked.

"Correct." My brother laughed.

After Marilyn hung up the phone, my mother and I finally could follow up on the news that my brother had hurt his arm. Charles answered lightly, "Yes, I hurt my arm when playing tennis. Don't worry. Didn't you hear Dad was with me?"

ஃ ஃ ஃ

My mother didn't talk much about her feelings after the séance. The next day, I saw her stepping outside of her room with a pair of sunglasses and a hat. I asked, "Mom, do you need to run errands? Would you like me to give you a ride?"

She shook her head and said, "Please do not follow me. I want to take a walk. Don't worry. I will be back when I finish walking."

She walked for an hour and a half. Starting from that day, I was grateful to see the long lost smile gradually reappear on my mother's face. After all, my mother realizes that she has to live the best of herself, to complete all of her tasks and be Su contentedly, because this is her only lifetime as Su.

My father's ashes had been transported to the United States and buried in a nearby cemetery. On April 5, 2003, I took my mother to my father's grave. As my father requested, we brought some red flowers. We also brought my father's favorite date cookies and my mother tasted one, as he had requested. Most Chinese bring food to their ancestors' cemeteries, as if the spirits would come to enjoy the food, but until my father communicated with us through Marilyn, I didn't realize the ritual did carry some meaning: Spirits cannot taste the food directly, but they can taste it through the living.

On that day my mother wore a dark red brocade jacket. It was a captivating deviation from the navy or black attire she had worn for three and a half years.

Connecting with My Mother-in-Law

Victor also arranged a family session to communicate with his late mother. On February 19, 2003, Victor and his father, Henry, initiated a three-way call from our house with two of Victor's sisters in Irvine, California, and Marilyn in Florida. I joined the phone conversation as an interpreter for my father-in-law. Prior to that call, we did not supply Marilyn with any information about Victor's mother or his family.

At the very beginning of the conversation, after Marilyn was introduced to everyone, she said, "I got a message that I don't understand what it means. I'm told it's in Chinese, but I don't read or speak Chinese. I kind of spelled it out phonetically. It came from a very strong lady. I believe this is Victor, Kelly, and Catherine's mother, but I'm not 100 percent sure. She says something that sounds like 'Wu' or 'Wo,' and—how do you pronounce A-I?"

"Like the word 'eye,'" I replied.

"And N-I? That's the message I'm supposed to give from her to Victor, Kelly, Catherine, and her husband, Henry. What does that mean?"

As an interpreter for my father-in-law, I answered Marilyn, "Wo Ai Ni (我愛你), I love you."

"Your mother-in-law spoke Chinese?"

"Yes, but she also spoke English."

"But she wanted me to get this across as I spelled it. I worked on it all morning with her. So that's the message for everyone listening."

This compelling phrase heavily knocked at the eardrums of each one of Victor's family because Sally had passed on suddenly of a heart attack in October 2001 without any dying words.

Marilyn first spoke to Kelly, who was pregnant with her second child. Marilyn said, "Your mother thanks you, Kelly, for praying for her. She felt your prayers. You talked to her this weekend?"

Kelly said, "I didn't say a prayer, but I did think of her."

Marilyn said, "She picked it up. And she sends this message: If it is possible, can you stick her name in the middle in the child's name?"

Kelly said, "Sure. Sally?"

"Would that be all right?"

"Sure."

"Do you know the sex of the child?"

"It's a girl."

"Right. Mom says, 'Not the first name. But somewhere in the middle.' Can you stick her name in?"

"Sure."

"I don't know if it's customary . . . Your mom says she hopes you don't mind if she doesn't hold your hands while you give birth. But she will be near you if that's OK."

"OK."

"She is telling you, Kelly, to make sure that you have your bags packed because you are going to give birth early. The baby is going to work out. Have more faith in what you do because your opinion is very important. You are not making any mistake. Don't worry about your mood swings. That's normal. She thinks you are very courageous."

Kelly's decision to have a second child was not easy. Her first child, Melodie, was already eight and Kelly was the owner of a small business. Kelly thanked Marilyn and said tremblingly, "My daughter, Melodie, wants to ask if she's OK. And Melodie misses her."

Marilyn said, "She knows that. Melodie sees her in her dreams. Your mother says Melodie says she sees her, correct?"

Kelly said, "Yes."

Marilyn explained, "Melodie is not lying. She is telling you the truth. Listen to what your daughter is telling you, because your mother has to come to see her. Please give Melodie the biggest hug and kiss you can, and tell her to continue to talk about 'Pa-Pa' or 'Po-Po.' I kept hearing these sounds. What does the sound mean?"

Kelly answered, "Po-Po (婆婆) means 'maternal grandma' in

Chinese. It is exactly what Melodie calls my mother."

As would happen a month later when Marilyn described my nephew Jason seeing my father, it was confirmed by the spirit of Sally that Melodie saw her. These two similar happenings made me wonder about what adults have been instructed to tell youngsters regarding spirits. Perhaps many of us could see or hear the spirits when we were young, but we learned to pay no attention to the phenomenon and lost the ability forever after we were corrected by the adults with whom we shared our experience.

Marilyn next spoke to Catherine, saying, "Studying is very strong with you, Catherine. You were excellent at school. You strove to be the best, but not loudly. Quietly. Your mother remembers your first son, Eric, very well. She says he has a very sweet personality. She's telling me that he may not be the best athlete in the world, and sometimes he may get quietly rebellious. He internalizes a lot. Your mother is saying he is artistic and supersensitive."

"Eric is indeed artistic and sensitive," Catherine agreed.

"Your mom is saying, 'Just leave him alone.' Give him more creative work to do. And it's just not on paper. He is creative with numbers, too. You cannot crush his artistic ability. You may have to put him into a special school or do homeschooling for him to grow in the field that he is good at."

Like most Chinese parents, Catherine wanted her son to excel at school. She emphasized the value of study to Eric, but Eric had his own philosophy and just did not listen to her. It worried Catherine that Eric did not like school. Yet she could not imagine homeschooling him because she got mad at Eric frequently. "Besides, what would Mother think?" Catherine sometimes asked herself.

When Sally was young, she passed a very competitive college entrance exam and entered the Mathematics Department in the well-respected Taiwan University. Unfortunately, her father's business failed when she was a sophomore. Even though she was the best of the twelve siblings at school, Sally had no choice but to drop out of college and start working. Because of her own regret, she put high emphasis on study when teaching her own children. But Marilyn brought a new perspective from Sally to Catherine: "Even though when she was flesh she would be yelling, she doesn't feel that way anymore. What she is stressing now is allowing the family to grow the way it's supposed to, and everyone should stop interfering.

"Your mother is saying you are following the traditional route. Everything you are trying to do is correct, but it's not correct for him. Your mother appreciates your opinion, but in this particular case, he should be given different kind of work. He is not going to grow out of this. It will grow deep underneath the surface, and it will still have to come through at some point in his life. Let him know that he can study and create at the same time. Give him the tools so that he takes the creative thoughts and puts them into the academics. Your mother wants me to tell you, if you are buying him a design set and things that are around buildings to build up, he will love it, because it's all art. And at the same time it will force him to learn mathematics and reading. So you are giving him an option of learning what it is to create. Make sure he studies, but don't be mean to him. Your mother is saying he has the ability to create. Don't let it go to waste. Let him paint freely. Just keep buying him things to draw and paint on, and say, 'This would look wonderful on a building like this, how would you design it?'"

Catherine was quietly puzzled, thinking, "Is this right? Does this kind of talk really come from my mother?"

Marilyn answered her thought, "She says of course when she was alive, she wouldn't behave this way. She would be demanding. But she says she is seeing things from a different angle."

Marilyn continued to speak to Sally's husband and children: "Your mother says, 'The family we have together, I am extremely proud of.' She did trust her husband's opinion in life. She thought he was a good husband. He is kinder than she was. She remembers the sweetness of his nature, especially when he was young and shy. She now says, 'I apologize for demanding a lot from him.' She asks for her husband's forgiveness. She also apologizes this to all of her children for the same thing. She had to be stronger than he many times. She had to come across with that strength in her voice. She knows that she has hurt him. For that she is sorry. She offended him in front of the children and it shows a lack of respect. But she didn't mean that. If she had to do life all over again, it would begin with her husband—she felt she might have been too rude to him at times."

Upon hearing the Chinese interpretation, Henry laughed and said in Chinese for me to interpret in English, "Don't worry about it. I completely understand."

Since I met my mother-in-law only once before her passing, I did not understand the significance of her spirit describing herself as "demanding a lot." After the session my father-in-law explained to me, "I was a captain in the navy first. Then I changed my job to be a commercial liner captain. Most of the time I was not home. Fortunately my wife was strong and capable of educating our children and dealing with the daily activities. Deep in my heart, I really appreciated her being strong. When I came home, if she lost her temper, I would not be angry. I wanted my children to be considerate toward my wife. It is hard to be a captain's wife."

Marilyn continued, "Your father is sensible. Don't be hard on him."

Catherine asked, "What do you mean?"

Marilyn said, "Your mother wants you to understand he has to live his life, too, even though you may have questions about certain things that he is doing. She wants him to know that his family will always take care of him. She also wants him to know that she approves of him having love: She [the new love] is younger than he. Your mother wants him to be happy. He needs that. It's perfectly normal for him to have another wife if he wants to. She doesn't want her son or daughters to interfere in his love life. He will be much nicer to all of you if you don't interfere. I was getting embarrassed to deliver the message— She says, 'But be wise and be frugal.' She understands his back has been bothering him. Make sure his new girlfriend massages his back."

Henry laughed loudly when he heard the interpretation. Then Marilyn said, "He is laughing—that's what she wants him to do."

The Chu family was astonished. Two weeks before the session, Victor and his sisters found out their father was determined to marry a lady who was much younger than he. Henry got to know this lady, Judy, in China through a friend in Taiwan who had recently married Judy's best friend. Henry and Judy had never met. They exchanged letters for three months and had seen one picture of each other through their mutual friends. Henry's children were concerned about his decision for several reasons. They thought the decision was too casual. They also wondered about this Chinese lady's motivation to marry an eighty-year-old man in the United States. Would she be nice to their father? What was he doing? Was he so lonely since their mother died that he had become gullible? Could he not find a lady friend suitable for his age in the local community? All these questions and concerns made the family worry. Henry, on the other hand, was hurt that his children did not respect his choice and trust his decision. The children had a heated private debate with their father and had not reached a conclusion or a solution before Sally asked Marilyn to deliver her message.

ॐ ॐ ॐ

The message about Kelly's second daughter was important because Kelly's first child had been born after the due date, and Sally apparently wanted to prepare Kelly for an easier birth this time. Two weeks after the family session with Marilyn, Kelly gave an easy natural birth to her second daughter, Elaine—before her due date. In memory of her own mother, Kelly used Sally as Elaine's middle name.

Although Elaine never saw her grandmother Sally, she is certainly adored by Sally. The day after Elaine's second birthday in 2005, while changing Elaine's diaper, Kelly smelled a strong, sweet flower scent. But no flowers were around. This sort of floral fragrance when no flowers were around had happened three times since Sally passed away. This time, she thought the scent was from an orchid flower pin in the master bedroom. She said to Elaine, "Wow! Your birthday gift smells good!"

After Kelly put Elaine to bed and went back to the master bedroom, she asked her husband if he smelled the flowers. He was confused and said no. Kelly smelled the orchids, but there was no scent at all.

Kelly knew that Sally had visited her. It was a gift from Sally.

Catherine had been bothered by the fact that her son Eric

had been playing with Legos all the time. His self-indulgence with Legos drove her mad and caused her to worry about his basic skills. The communication with her mother made her realize that she was making herself too nervous over his toy. She learned from Sally that she had to respect his talents and guide him accordingly. Catherine gradually loosened her control over Eric. She watched him and let him do whatever he wanted, but firmly set the limits. Her minimum requirement was that he achieve straight As in school. Adjusting her way of disciplining Eric became the key to the change of their relationship. Eric and Catherine can joke with each other now spontaneously. And, to Catherine's surprise, Eric has achieved straight As in a class for gifted children since 2004.

As for their relationship with their father, Catherine, Kelly, and Victor felt vigorously refreshed after the family séance. They realized that they should treat him as an adult rather than a child. They decided that they should listen to their mother's words and not interfere with their father's new love life. Consequently, they chose to help their father to have a pleasant trip to China to visit his lady friend and get to know her face-to-face. The two were married in 2005.

Linking Uncle Liang-Yuan

My mother, Su, and Marilyn met only once, in 2003. Since then, they have always sent regards to each other through me. Every time I talk to Marilyn, she asks about my mother, and my mother frequently asks about Marilyn. I feel that their care for each other is neither a way of showing courtesy to me nor mere lip service.

When she is asked about her impression of Marilyn by her friends, my mother answers, "Marilyn is very down to earth." Then with a sweet smile, she always adds her own creative description, "Marilyn is like a Chinese. She is *very* Chinese."

I do not refute my mother's words in front of her friends. But I always thought it was strange for my mother to comment so.

Just before Christmas in 2004, Victor and I visited Marilyn to discuss about the details of this book. One night while we were reviewing the acknowledgments for this book, Marilyn spotted my mother's name among an alphabetical list of people I wanted to thank. Marilyn insisted on moving my mother's name to a front section and thanking my mother personally. Marilyn added that she felt closely connected to my mother. She said, "I want to cry with your mom and laugh with your mom."

I was shocked to hear that. They only met once, didn't they?

The next night, while dining opposite Victor and me in a booth at Denny's, Marilyn suddenly said to me, "I see a man's face on you."

Victor and I looked at each other, not understanding. Then we saw Marilyn stare at me. Her face was emotionless; her eyes were wide open and moist. She appeared to be going into a trance.

Marilyn continued describing this man's face: "The shape of his face is not like yours. His is round. Also his face has lots of pimples."

I thought I knew who this man might be, but I needed more information from her to confirm, so I asked Marilyn, "What else do you see?"

"Now he is writing English letters on your forehead. Wait. Let me see it once more. It is Y-U-A-N. Does this make sense to you?"

Tears were flowing down my cheeks. I could barely answer her question: "It is my eldest uncle."

ఎ ఎ ఎ

Ever since Marilyn told me in our first phone conversation in 2002 that my father said that he was with my uncle, I felt sorry that I did not have any message from my eldest uncle, Liang-Yuan (良元), to my mother or my grandmother. My eldest uncle and my mother were raised in the country by their grandmother. They were very close to each other and shared many memories.

My grandmother used to be like an empress among her family and friends. When my mother decided to run away with my father, my grandmother would not allow any of my uncles to visit my mother. The day before my parents' wedding, taking the risk of being punished by his own mother, Uncle Liang-Yuan paid my mother a brief, furtive visit and gave her his blessings. Then he rushed back so that his mother wouldn't find out that he had disobeyed her.

The relationship between my mother and Uncle Liang-Yuan was so trusting that she is still proud of it. Furthermore, my grandmother also missed Uncle Liang-Yuan very much. She kept saying that he was the most filial child in the family. So I wished I could bring some message from him to them.

Just as I had done with my father's spirit, two weeks before my trip to Florida to meet Marilyn, I decided to communicate with Uncle Liang-Yuan at my heart. I said to him, "Eldest uncle, will you come to me? Will you show me some proof that it is you if you come? Do you have messages you want me to deliver?" I silently sent the message to him for two weeks without letting Victor or Marilyn know about it.

My uncle had indeed had a round face. Because of the prescriptions he had to take all his life to keep his severe asthma in control, his face was bloated. The prescriptions also made his face full of pimples, even in adulthood. When I was young,

I sometimes looked at my uncle's moon face and thought it peculiar, because he was the only adult I had ever met who had a face full of pimples.

❧ ❧ ❧

So I knew it was my uncle when I heard Marilyn's description of the face. Even though I had invited him, his appearance was still a surprise to me. I asked Marilyn, "What does my uncle want to say?"

Marilyn relayed that he felt divorcing his wife had been a mistake. There was no fault on her side. He loved her. She was good to him in every way, including in the bedroom. He had quarreled with her in front of his mother because he wanted to show that he was in control. He was sorry that he had broken up the family and said he was fully responsible. What he should have done was run away with his family instead of following his mother's orders, but he did not have the courage. He said he'd had enough of Chinese traditions. He wanted to have more romance in the next life, so he would be a French man enjoying life without children.

I could not control the tears rushing down my cheeks. Only my uncle Liang-Yuan could have said these words through Marilyn.

❧ ❧ ❧

Uncle Liang-Yuan's life was a tragedy. He was born with severe asthma. Then, at age three, he was crippled by polio. He remained very short after the polio strike, and his appearance was not handsome at all.

My mother had an excellent relationship with Uncle Liang-Yuan's wife. She appreciated the fact that my aunt did not mind his handicaps. My aunt also treated my mother well. She knit sweaters for my mother, and when she visited her family in the country, she was usually kind enough to bring fresh fruits or vegetables to my mother.

On the other hand, the relationship between my grandmother and my uncle's wife was contentious. First, as a highly educated woman in her generation, my grandmother totally disagreed with her son's marriage because her daughter-in-law had only a primary-school education. In her generation in China it was important, especially for the oldest son, that a matrimonial alliance was established between families of similar class, and my grandmother believed this shortcoming made the family lose face. Moreover, finances caused other conflicts between my aunt and my grandmother.

Even with his disability, Uncle Liang-Yuan was a loyal son to the Lee family. As the eldest son, he contributed one-third of his salary to his mother to lessen her financial burden. My grandmother was the only breadwinner and carried the load for the ten-member family for a long time after my grandfather permanently lost his job and became chronically ill. After Uncle Liang-Yuan married, he continued contributing one-third of his salary to his mother. As the result, his own family had to live a financially limited life. My aunt started arguing with him privately. In the meantime, when my grandmother visited Uncle Liang-Yuan, he told his wife to treat his mother luxuriously. His wife's pride would not allow to betray that they usually lived frugally, either. Since my grandmother loved to eat fish, my aunt bought the most expensive fish in the market and cooked extra dishes. But her hospitality earned only my grandmother's contempt and concern.

Even though my grandmother had been carefree in her early married years, she had to budget meticulously and carefully for a long time after 1949. When my grandmother saw the rich meals prepared especially for her, she did not understand how the daughter-in-law could be so extravagant. She was worried that my aunt didn't know how to make ends meet.

Their financial situation did not improve, and my uncle and aunt quarreled frequently. After their quarrels, she frequently went to stay with her maiden family. One time while she was away, their five-year-old son broke his arm. Uncle Liang-Yuan had to bring his son to work because he could not afford a babysitter. This kind of thing occurred so many times that my grandmother became vigorous in her efforts to convince her son to divorce his own wife.

Under pressure from his mother, Uncle Liang-Yuan finally divorced his wife. At that time, the law in Taiwan specified that custody of children went to the father. Besides, from my grandmother's perspective, her former daughter-in-law was an unfit mother who couldn't be a normal role model for the young grandchildren.

After the divorce, Uncle Liang-Yuan raised his children on his own. Sometimes he had to bring the children to work with him, and he became a laughingstock among his colleagues. Nevertheless, he continued to support his mother financially until he died at age fifty-five, just after his children entered the workforce.

Uncle Liang-Yuan's divorce was a taboo in the Lee household. My other uncles never mentioned the divorce or the ex-wife. We were all smart enough to not touch the sensitive subject. Even my mother did not talk about it with us. So I was surprised that my mother suddenly mentioned it in November 2004, just one month before Marilyn saw my uncle's face on mine.

"I am still angry with Uncle Liang-Yuan's ex-wife," my mother casually said to me while we were window-shopping on a sunny day.

"Why?" I asked.

"When they first divorced, I thought they did it to temporarily calm your grandma down. After all, I thought, when your grandmother became older, perhaps they could reunite themselves. I did not expect your ex-aunt to immediately remarry. It was hard for a man to raise two children, especially a man with weak physical condition like your uncle's. Besides, how could she agree to divorce? Didn't she care for her children? I used to be friends with her. But that was long time ago."

Hearing these words, I awkwardly ended the conversation with silence—I did not know how to quench my mother's heat.

❧ ❧ ❧

Now, one month after my mother's first discussion with me about my uncle's divorce, Uncle Liang-Yuan apparently wanted to reopen the case and give his ex-wife the credit she was due.

I asked Marilyn, "Does my uncle have other messages for me to deliver? What about his mother, my grandmother?"

"Well, he said earlier he takes the full responsibility for his failed marriage and does not blame anybody else. As for your grandma, he respects her, but he does not miss her. He does not have a message for her."

At first I felt sad. I had thought all the spirits came back to be sweet. Why was this time different?

To me, my grandmother is like a bottle of wine which ages so well that it becomes a collector's item. Despite that she lost her father at her early childhood; her husband, middle age; her eldest son, old age, she ultimately survived the losses with dignity. At the age of ninety, my amiable grandmother embraces her life more and more gracefully and displays the wisdom toward people. She is so warm and kind that every member in her Tai Chi club befriends her, and many of them are thirty to forty years younger than she is. They like to share their stories with her because she is open-minded and always willing to help.

But I soon remembered that Eileen had said all people have karma. Perhaps it was Uncle Liang-Yuan's and his mother's karma. Who was I to judge?

As I recalled Eileen's words in my head, Marilyn said, "This man also wants to write or draw." She asked for a pen and a piece of paper. Then she started sketching while looking at me. She tried several times. Then she pushed her work to me and sighed, "It's hard."

I looked at the paper and realized that Marilyn, who did not know how to write Chinese, had just copied the Chinese characters of my uncle's name, Liang-Yuan (良元). I recognized "Yuan" immediately, but it took me a few minutes to decipher "Liang" because Marilyn did not know those strokes were supposed to be a character. But the strokes were in perfectly correct order for me to identify the character!

I told Marilyn, "I am thankful. He showed his proof."

Then Marilyn said, "He is not finished with you yet. Oh, and he is telling me that your mother and I were sisters."

"You and my mother? When and where?"

"Yes, Su and I. We were on an icy mountain somewhere on the border of China and Russia in the 800s. He said at that time only men could eat meat; women could not. People used horns to communicate. Oh, isn't this wonderful? No wonder I feel so close to your mother!"

We were all amazed to finally discover the answers to the mysterious chemistry between Marilyn and my mother. We were all related. It was not an accident. Perhaps my mother and Marilyn needed me to meet each other in this lifetime. Perhaps we all agreed before we became mortal.

Since this unusual discovery, I see people differently and

I have more patience toward others. I don't know what kind of lesson I will learn from any individual I meet, but I believe there may be a predestined connection between him or her and me, and I am happy to see the lesson of this lifetime unfold. I would like to do my best and establish good karma for the next lifetime.

ə⍺ ə⍺ ə⍺

Before I had personal séance experience, I did not believe "I love you" had a real meaning. I thought it was the cheapest token Westerners gave their family and friends. Now I have completely changed my view. I figured that if it is so important that the spirits would return just to stress this message, why should we hesitate to express these words while our physical bodies are still alive?

During my childhood, my parents never missed any of my school anniversaries or PTA meetings even though both had busy careers. Now, of course, I understand that they cared about me so much that they wanted to keep updated with my school. But back then, I thought their close involvement with my school activities made me look childish. Many of my classmates' parents were too busy to show up. I thought those classmates were cool and hip. So whenever my parents were at my school, I showed them a dim face instead of appreciation. My parents' presence was an embarrassment to me at a time when my peers appeared detached and independent.

This time is different. I am proud and courageous to let people know that my father's spirit was and still is here. Marilyn successfully delivered his message and the messages of others, and through her work I learn that love can surpass the boundary of physical demise and the language barrier.

13

The Beat Goes On

At sixty, my ear was an obedient organ for the reception of the truth.

—Confucius (551–479 BCE)

THE FOUNDATION FOR becoming a psychic/medium was carefully measured and laid out in my youth. From the starting point and through a few years of absence before it resurfaced, this incredible journey had often confounded and confused me—but it always blessed my life with an abundance of awareness and love. In spite of the rough journey, often filled with people who tried to discourage my work and an attitude in society that makes fun of folks like me or labels us as crazy, it has been an honor to serve my friends in the spirit world and help those mortals who seek us out.

Deep within my sensing, I have grown to believe that perhaps we all do choose our lives before we enter into them. Maybe my map-out is to be and do what I have grown into. And maybe the obstacles placed on my journey are there to keep me on my toes and help me become wiser as I gather more knowledge and awareness.

Does it really matter whether or not I am consciously aware of asking to do this work? The answer is clearly no. Does it matter whether or not it came to me in my youth? Clearly, no. Do those who started out earlier have an advantage over those seeking it in their adulthood? Absolutely not.

In my humble opinion, all people, whenever they decide to stir and awaken their natural-born talents in the arena of the paranormal, can develop and use their gifts. Not all are going to become the greatest, or even any good at all, but many will feel very rewarded in learning much about a subject that has until recently been considered a taboo. With comprehension and understanding, one's mind and heart soften, and a compassion filled with patience, tolerance, and love emerges. The knowledge gathered makes for a more harmonious life. Being in the service of the spirits continues to be a blessing in my daily life.

Thoughts regarding whether these spirit entities are really who they say they are, or are an extension of me, plagued my life for many years. The years I spent questioning turned out to be a growing process. Once convinced that I should examine and explore my mediumistic ability, things began to take shape and my road was set. I made a commitment to do this work, regardless of the many obstacles and challenges, hits and misses that could occur.

I was lucky enough to have my angelic friends to hold my hand and guide me through this formidable task. I am not religious, yet one named James, a brother of Yeshua, is my control and has been guiding me throughout my life. Nor was I seeking attention via mediumship, yet one named Eileen is my wise teacher. The spirit of June demonstrates holistic health to me. Hemingway led me to understand and appreciate guts and passion about life. Each of them has their own distinctive essential expertise that becomes their own imprints. A very special thank you goes to my beloved James, Eileen, and June—and, of course, Papa, too. Without my angelic friends, I truly believe that all of what I do would not be possible.

Through my deep-trance states to lightly altered states of consciousness, many entities, especially James and Eileen, have communicated through me. They have offered solace and love to many. The healing that has resulted is a treasured, precious gift. With delicate cheers they acknowledge our lives. What is actually taking place in a medium's psyche, I do not know. But I do know that what motivates me to constantly learn, grow, and share is the ability to provide healing to suffering people. Being able to see these people alleviate their sorrow and anguish is a very great reward.

Appendix A

Psychic Development 101

This is indeed firmly grounded when it is persistently exercised for a long time, without interruption, and with earnest, reverential attention and devotion.
—Yoga Sutras I:14

WE ARE SPIRITS in human bodies. Therefore, we have built-in psychic capabilities. But these capabilities may be dormant or suppressed. One can awaken them and open them up by doing certain exercises and by following a good teacher. This appendix explores some of the exercises I teach to my students. These are the most fundamental but also the most important exercises for psychic development.

You may call these exercises Psychic Development 101. But remember, Psychic Development 101 is the same as Psychic Development 201 and Psychic Development 301: Keep practicing and you will get there.

Breathing and Relaxation Exercise

Breathing is the most important aspect of all the psychic exercises. It relaxes your body and your mind. Light meditation with deep breathing helps the mind facilitate communication. The exercise is as follows.

- Get into your most comfortable position and loosen anything that is tight. Close your eyes and relax.

- Flex your toes, then relax.

- Tighten your calves, then relax.

- Tighten your stomach, then relax.

- Take a long, deep, slow breath through your nose and slowly exhale through your mouth, and relax. Repeat this four times.

- Make a fist with your right hand, then relax.

- Make a fist with your left hand, then relax.

- Roll your shoulders forward, then relax.

- Roll your shoulders backward, then relax.

- Stretch your face muscles, then relax.

- Take a long, slow, deep breath through your nose and slowly exhale through your mouth, and relax. Repeat this four times.

- Slowly drop your head down, then over to your left shoulder, then all the way back, then over to your right shoulder. Then drop your head all the way down, back to the right, gently to the back, over to the left, then all the way down. Repeat this three times. Then drop your head all the way down, slowly lift it up and drop it all the way back, then lift it up and relax.

- Feel all the tenseness leave your body, breathe slowly, and relax.

- Keep your eyes closed. Slowly inhale through your nose and exhale through your mouth. Do this five times.

- Using the same rhythm of inhaling and exhaling, slowly inhale through your nose to the count of five, then slowly exhale through your mouth to the count of five. Do this five times.

- Gently reduce the speed of your breathing. Slowly inhale through your nose to the count of five, retain to the count of five, and exhale to the count of five. Do the same for the counts of four, three, two, and one. Count down using the same rhythm while breathing in and out.

Chakra-Opening Exercise

Chakras are centers of awareness. There are seven major charkras in our body:

- Top of the head

- Center of the forehead (the third eye)

- Throat

- Heart

- Solar plexus

- Navek

- Base of the spine

The key to opening the chakras is breathing and relaxed concentration. You will need to take deep breaths, inhaling, and exhaling slowly, while concentrating on the chakras.

First, close your eyes, get into your most comfortable position, and relax. Then do five rounds of the breathing exercise using the five down to one count as follows:

- Inhale to the count of five.

- Hold to the count of five while concentrating on the top of your head chakra.

- Upon exhaling, chant "OM . . . " It should resonate like a soothing, soft, melodic sound, beginning with "OOOOO" and ending in "MMMMM" until you are out of breath.

- Continue to do the same for the center of your forehead, throat, heart, solar plexus, navel, and base of your spine.

Some of the sensations you may experience during the opening of these seven centers of awareness are heat, coolness, tingling, light-headedness, and other subtle differences to your body.

Self-Healing Exercise

After doing these breathing exercises, you are ready to begin your journey into psychic development.

- Do the breathing and chakra-opening exercises.

- Keep your eyes closed and sit with the palms of your hands facing the ceiling. Slowly raise your hands until they are over your head, with palms still facing the ceiling.

- Take slow, deep breaths and feel the energy gather into the center of each hand.

- Hold your hands there until it feels completely different and you feel tingling.

- Slowly lower your hands and place them on any part of your body that is hurting you. Always place your right hand on the spot first, then your left hand over it.[1]

- Stay that way for a minute or so, allowing the self-healing to flow until the tingling sensation is gone from the center of each palm.

- Then open your eyes and relax.

All of the above exercises take about fifteen to twenty minutes. The next step involves actual psychic development exercises to develop different facets of psychic ability.

Telepathy Exercises

Telepathy is mind-to-mind communication without the use of speech or body language. It is "one of the vital functions, and a mastery of its potentialities will enormously enrich the personality and experience of any individual who learns to use it" (Garrett 1945).

The following exercises will help you to awaken your telepathic faculty.

---

[1] The spirits ask that in a self-healing, we honor the living flesh before the spirits, because it is important that we feel our life force first, before theirs is added to it. To do this, we place the right hand on a wounded area and the left hand over it because the right hand signifies the living and the left hand signifies the spirit. If an injured person is unable to place the right hand on the wounded area, however, it's acceptable to simply place the left hand directly on the wound.

Game 1

- Two people should sit opposite each other and hold hands.

- Eyes remain open throughout this exercise.

- The partners choose who will be partner 1 and who will be partner 2. They remain as 1 and 2 throughout the exercise.

- Partner 1 goes first and mentally sends a vision of a body part from the waist up. Partner 1 sends it for about ten seconds and then releases partner 2's hands. Partner 2 tells partner 1 of her findings.

- The partners then hold hands again and partner 2 mentally sends partner 1 a vision of a body part from the waist down. Partner 2 sends it for about ten seconds and then releases partner 1's hands. Partner 1 tells partner 2 of her findings.

- The above exercise can be done using many different mental images, as long as they are within the same category. One can send a vision of a number from 1 to 10, a location in Europe, a geometric shape, a season, a fruit, a vegetable, and so on. The possibilities are endless. This form of telepathy is fun to do and helps build up confidence in the sender and receiver. Five to seven rounds is usually enough to start the evening.

Game 2

- Send someone out of the room while the rest of the group concentrates upon a body part of that student.

- Upon returning, the person will focus in on where the group's energies are directing him to sense. Both senders and receivers may take up to a full minute before the receiver makes a statement.

- One may feel a tingling, heat, cold, or gentle vibration in the area the group is focusing upon.

Game 3

- One individual says the first name of someone, alive or passed. The rest of the group senses things about the person whose name that was spoken.

The above three exercises should take about an hour to complete.

Psychometry Exercises

Psychometry is the ability to retrieve information about people or events by touching associated objects.

Game 1

- Pair off and exchange items: a watch, ring, a necklace, a set of keys, or anything that is easily removed.

- Have your partner hold an item of yours for a minute and then tell you a story about the item, or about yourself or something pertaining to your life.

Game 2

- Each member of the group writes down his or her name on a piece of paper.

- Fold the paper, then put it into a bowl. Everyone's folded paper should look exactly alike.

- Each person then takes one paper out of the bowl, but no one should unfold the paper until everyone in the group has had a chance to tell what they feel of the person whose name they have selected.

This is a fun-filled exercise because often people give elaborate thoughts pertaining to the person whose name they must read. Sometimes upon opening the paper up they laugh realizing they have read themselves. On a serious side, many reveal good psychic news to each other.

A typical exercise in psychometry will take about twenty minutes.

Telekinesis Exercises

Telekinesis is the ability to move physical objects without touching them.

Game 1

- Hang something off a lamp, pole, or anything that doesn't move and is not affected by wind.

- Have everyone focus on the item and use their energy to will it to move. Everyone must be in unison regarding which way the object should sway.

Game 2

- Place a toothpick on a table.

- Have everyone sit around it and focus on making it move.

These exercises should take about an hour of deep concentration.

ꝫ ꝫ ꝫ

The above exercises are some of the things offered in a typical psychic development workshop. In total, the evening should last three to five hours. I offer simple exercises here because I believe that when you achieve hits, it encourages you to go further and transfer your wins to daily life.

The exercises help open up your mind to allow yourself to build confidence and a positive connection when doing psychic work. The more exercises one does in psychic development, the better he or she gets at it. It also is the acceptance of our brain that allows this activity to take place. I feel it also helps to shed any negativity that one may have about being psychic and fosters health in mind, body, and spirit.

Appendix B

Writing by Spirits

*The Tao that can be described is not the enduring and
unchanging Tao. The name that can be spoken is not
the enduring and unchanging name.*

—Lao Tzu (c. sixth century BCE)

ATTAINING ONE FULL page of writing from the spirits can take
upward of five hours. I do not correct a thought expressed by
them, even if it sounds incorrect to me. Getting the flow going
and the information out is more important than fussing over
grammar, syntax, and style. The language pattern is theirs,
and the intent is to convey messages. The entities of James
and Eileen come to me as writers.

Eileen wrote much on the subject of mediumship and being
psychic: an examination of herself and endless experiments
she was involved with, and her personal struggles in life and
how she overcame these major obstacles. Her accomplish-
ments and contributions to the field of parapsychology surpass
those of any other woman, past or present. She astounded
many when mortal, including prestigious people from the sci-

entific community. To date, via my trances, she continues to captivate her audiences. Her generosity and consideration for us all is extraordinary. She explains how when one arrives in heaven, he or she evolves to a higher thought, and words she once used to express her sentiments have changed and her old awareness has become enhanced. Whenever she can write about *talking*, she uses me.

Both entities are phenomenal in their own right. They bring to a séance their love, wit, and knowledge. In my humble opinion, they are a gift to all they touch.

A Showcase of Colors

The Spirit of Eileen J. Garrett

Eileen asked me to write down the meaning of colors from a spirit's perspective. Here is what she had to say.

Yellow This color reminds me of work. It resembles feelings associated with remembering work. It takes on a whirl of light that resounds in sound. It contains a home of love. The feeling of yellow is calming. It has many aspects to it. Light that emanates from it can caress a soul and make it feel soothed. Sounds are very often happy, they relate to a happy sense.

From where we speak, the collective form of yellow is brilliant in our thoughts. Thus, brilliance shine[s] for all of us when we feel the color yellow. We all recall feelings of happiness and people loving yellow. To create the sense for this, we remember things that were yellow.

From where I live, yellow is my vision of lowlands and light. For us here, this color is very alive, as if it were a form of life. Our connected collective thoughts of yellow create yellow.

Orange Color orange connects to a thought of careful placed lights. It resounds with constant forces of "Look, here I am." This contact with common careful placed lights regards our life from a dial of love.

Orange is available to those who like people. This is a friendly color that we relate to the sense of autumn. It takes on a life of light that connects in our collective thoughts. The sound that emanates from orange is similar to a playground filled with laughing children at play. The sense we gather from this color is whimsical in nature and filled with everlasting gaiety. This color is a brilliant showcase.

Red Passion rises from red. We sense this color as being proud, alive with active movement. The connected collected feed on red spirals through all we sense. It is a color that is filled with power and proud passion.

Red makes me think of love. Oftentimes this was my connection to it. My feelings about red collect in my remembrance as it should, with emotions filled with merriment. The color red gives me a power that makes me feel good. In this world I reside in, I relate to red. High energy emanates from it. One can use it as a test for their passions. My heart is filled with a fond remembrance of this color. I love red. It knows I do and responds with love.

Blue The part of life we can sense and treat to our time is often collected in blue. Blue is associated with the power of God. Proud feelings filled with biblical tales are always connected to blue. Its fragrance reminds us of hope, of people gathering in religious places. Each place distinct in its aroma. Each group of people enriched with the scent of blue.

A collective feeling about blue is old and honored. Wisdom of ages and tales of light are powered by this color. It becomes our guiding light whenever we pull it into our thoughts for purposes of growing. Rays of this color collect in all of us and we feel high from them.

Green I recall this color as one often associated with healing. From my field in Paradise, green is alive with wealth. It collects my hand in knowing thoughts. Through green we care for people. We open to them through the many shades of green. Especially those beings who regard themselves as healers.

Green means Mecca (the Highest). Powers that emanate from green are ruled by Mecca. The green color is beautiful. It is alive with the power of love, nurturing all that exists. Proud feelings relate to this color. Honor, trust, compassion, truth, and all manner of proud forms belong to green. Green is a feeling of love. We result in feeding it to our living.

Indigo This is a sense of life with answers to it. Very much alive and filled with the knowing of all there is to grow with. In sharing this color we collect our way and remember work of all our past lives. This color works equal to the work of man. Meaning the power from this color represents work. We here work remembering our past lives, present circumstances and future existence's. Mainly past lives are involved with this color. In part it is the thought of this color and when contacting it we remember. Indigo represents power to recall. Indigo is a power to grow from, collecting a connecting power of love.

Violet A color we seldom feel for here. Having various connections to other colors it fragments our take on ruling our thoughts. We complete this shade with higher personal senses. Many here remember it in association with coming home. The hues vary to a deep purple giving the sensing for multitudes of souls here to recall connecting to their death.

Animals here are surrounded in violet. It fills them with love. Higher feelings created by the connected collective thoughts work with colors. They all possess a vibrational field that resonates with loving sound. Violet has its sound akin to a symphony playing in perfect harmony to one's deepest emotional feelings.

More on Colors

The Duo Team

The following thoughts about colors were offered by James and Eileen on August 18, 1999.

An ailing old man came pounding on my door.
I asked him what he needed and he said *Blue*.
I learned that *Blue* is the keeper of ancients and wisdom.

A sweet little girl asked for my help.
I asked what she needed and she told me *Orange*.
I learned that *Orange* is the door to gaiety.

A handyman offered me help.

I said I need none and he answered you certainly do.

He gave me *Red*, and I learned of passion.

A housewife asked for aid.

I offered her reason and she asked for *Green*.

I learned that *Green* was from Mecca.

And powers from life of life is what she needed.

A snob of a lady beckoned my hand to help her.

I offered her *Yellow* to gently calm and caress her soul.

An errand boy delivered my food.

I offered him *Violet* as payment.

I learned that *Violet* was for his winning ways with animals.

Here in heaven, the Son of greatness came barging into our house.

He offered us *Indigo*.

And we began our journeys on how to grow.

Is Life a Collection of Past Lives?

The Spirit of Eileen J. Garrett

Inviting me to regard that thought, remembering how many lives I did have, will remain Holy, forever in my love. These are the thoughts that root in me. We remember because our days are filled with working. Our work deals with dwelling in thoughts. When our power grows, we create more love. We collect our thinking with power from this love.

This light of life resulted in peering openly at her love. My connection to meeting my love remembered all my lives, these were times of growing. We here must grow. Love is the open take on Life of Life. We here could never ever send out naughty thoughts that would result in hurting a human life. Where I reside, past lives collect love. To remember a past life, I regarded love and remembered all those times words meant so very much to my existence. In that life I used the things and people available to me. Words were my power. I wrote on difficult subjects relating to being a medium and psychic. From my perspective here, I served that life well.

I never was able to openly accept reincarnation. Nor the thought of past lives. My feelings about these subjects have changed. To borrow a thought I once used in that existence. "It is enough to deal in one lifetime, and I certainly didn't need other lifetimes to merge with my day." I remember that feeling quite well. Realizing if I had given into that thought, then I wouldn't be worthy of my work. Remembering how I used to excite others to work on their projects collects in memory and I have good tales to tell on that.

We here do say, "Each living is excited about its life." That thought means that people must remind themselves to be excited as to who they are. The living of one life accounts for another life. Past, present and future are mingled with that one existence. The connected feelings to each existence remains eternal. So one could say, I could be speaking from an ancient existence while simultaneously be speaking from a more recent or future one. Interlaced with my Eileen feed, I am aware of many more lives. The old Eileen cannot send her answers from just that existence. A corrected thought on that equals the honor of taking on more of who we are.

Is life a collection of past lives?

So when answers are given from a soul who came home, it remembers that life but contacts a dialing of several livings going on simultaneously and must adjust its thoughts to feel the passion from that one existence it is being called in to address.

The term Diaries of Light means that all humans dwell in light and gifts.

Each past life is a compliance to what the soul must learn. Seeing is a part of those existences. Severed from the thought of having a Past Life soothes a power (Life) so that this life focuses on the insulation of its take of living.

I used to strongly feel that if our days were spent remembering past lives and then using the information as a reason for current issues, then we would remain stagnant in our current lives. Of course I am aware of the good work by many and the positive results from those dealing with past life issues and correcting current problems as a result of this type of therapy.

So, again I did grow from where my last life let me sense. Here we sense many tests. These are from our highest soul that implements who we count as ours in a soul nucleus. Every living has its memory here. Not in a book, but in the collection of thinking of who they are. To connect to a collective thought meant to connect to a collection of thinking. The creative force of thoughts is soothing to all of us here. We have no difficult time. Thinking is our way.

People can no longer take the *Old hard Light* of communicating with Heaven. We here can feel the telephone morsel, hearing in thought the very thought of humans crying out to reach us. With elephant ears we all hear. Many people want to talk to us. Many here want to talk to you. The medium is the instrument we use to do this work. Past Lives Do Exist. Regard current living and certainly give it the best shot you can.

Collecting My Feelings toward Words

An Aspect of Eileen J. Garrett

The following paper was given to me by an aspect of Eileen, one early September morning in 1999.

The many people I have met remembered words came from my work. My female form remembered wins in talking. Using my feminine thoughts for the work with words became quietly honored with my hard work. People learned about who we connected to because as a writer, I chose my words carefully. Many mornings I would set the day, talking about my feelings and putting them down on paper. An odd bond fed my inspiration. Peering at that time, well it looks like I was good at my job.

Having talked to many people worked well for me. I never called out forces to young kids. Never would I accept them and often reminded them to live their life and hug love. Words were a business for my life. My expression of my words was perfect for my carefully placed thoughts. Every day of my existence I used words to connect to others. My books were easy to write because of my work. I resulted in treating each book with power. The power was love. From love, came words. And there were times my words were of a warning. I recall writing ... As I have said again and again, "Any subject in this field that I used to write about is dangerous if you enter into it without objective understanding of what you are doing and what you are searching for." So, for me to write on the subjects I chose, I used what I would like to think was objective reasoning and the words I chose became my tool to express it with.

If my work was busy, my collective thoughts would flow easily because people opened up to my words. I wrote about people, I wrote about me and I wrote about the subject I was in love with. I was happy. To Eileen, my feelings are so high. That life made my win powered by words.

Intellectually, there were cases I needed to understand. I, therefore, became interested and researched them out. My assumed role as a medium and psychic allowed me to go explore and use the approach of being objective to write about them. My own mediumistic ability was scrutinized by me. I accorded my life much writing to express these subjects. Trying to be as objective as one can when speaking of oneself, I often found my work helped me to collect words and write about these adventures.

Thoughts probed by me, collected and nested in me till words expressed them. I was neither a saint nor sinner and felt comfortable using my visions and senses to hope to bring about understanding. To do this I became humble and words were important to my life. Separating the chaff from the wheat is a difficult job at best and a hard task to complete. Using words helped to allow better awareness and to this I am higher in serving of love.

Matters on Losing Weight

The Spirit of Eileen J. Garrett

More often than not, I experienced a sudden gain in weight after doing trance work. My friendly entities were very much aware of the situation. Eileen remembered how it would sometimes affect her, too, and she understood exactly what I was speaking about. Here is a paper offering her thoughts about it.

As I recall my thoughts involved with feelings of wheeling and dealing for Paradise's feed, I look back and remember my female form. These gifts from heaven were kind words to my life, and I remember severing my form when I worked. It looked like I was gaining weight, especially after my work as a medium. The weight would collect and all my clothes wouldn't fit properly. Being a lady who always projected a chic look, I often wondered if this was characteristic of doing mediumistic work, and if all people doing this type of work paid a price in weight gain. I never thought to ask my control if this was true, but my suspicions about it were ever increasing.

From my present state of being in spirit form I can definitely answer this question. There is no doubt about it, all those who do trance mediumship work can anticipate a sudden weight gain that will cling to your body and last between one and three days depending upon one's metabolism. Further research from my feelings here do indicate that we can safely assure all trance mediums that this sudden weight gain also affects the lungs, heart and back of all who do this type of work. We keep Marilyn bandaged with our invisible wraps that we surround her body in and do help to alleviate certain physical problems. But we do not seem to have an affect upon the sudden water weight gain.

It is funny for me to say these things because I was always sensing water in me and I wasn't able to figure out why. Of course we will leave this exploration to the greater minds in science who will one day explore this matter and hopefully come up with a solution to this problem.

I believe I know a way for the medium I use to lose the water weight quickly. I have been sensing her through our work together and do feel all she must do is indicate water weight will not be allowed to linger. Realizing these words are simply put and hard to trust in, from my perspective it does boil down to asking for weight gain during séance sessions to dissipate quickly. Unlike channelers, trance mediums do have a price to pay with their bodies. A host of other weight issues must not be confused with the sudden gain from trance work.

The question remains unanswered by mortals. However, I feel strong as to what I just indicated and believe it is as simple as asking oneself to not allow the water gain from trance work to reside and linger. I am asking my medium to put effort in this request to put it to a test.

As regards weight lose of a different kind which stems from dieting, etc., as a collective thought on this subject we here feel your science is approaching an era when mankind will no longer be held prisoner by overweight bodies. Yes, there will be a day in your future that being overweight will never be an issue.

We all feel that for those who do trance work, that gaining weight isn't always from working with us, but do take note that many females do have this occur.

My collection of thoughts regarding fasting . . . other than for personal reasons that one chooses to fast before going into a trance state, I do not feel it necessary for anyone to fast in order to connect to guides. For that matter I insist that people eat a proper balanced diet and toss out their thoughts of fasting as a requirement before communicating with their guides. All here share in these thoughts.

As one who used to communicate when in mortal female form, I realize that water weight gain, as unpleasant as it sometimes gets, doesn't have to be part of mediumistic work if people allow their thoughts to block it. We will be using Marilyn as a test for this issue.

Instead of the old belief that water gain is part and parcel to being a medium, we would prefer to challenge this by experimenting and having a cause and effect test set-up. To do this we are using Marilyn as our subject.

A Church Is Gifted

James, Dictated to Eileen

Eileen asked me to write it down this paper in 1999. It was dictated to Eileen from James. It is a compilation of James's thoughts that he once gave to me in the 1970s.

In my assumed role as a Hebrew, my life was consumed by Power from God. Involved in that friendly world were people who realized that periods of love were able to create the purpose for Yeshua. My brother was a kind king, anointed by a female and following a rather uncommon way of delivering God.

He was programmed from before birth. His simplistic way of speaking reached multitudes and he quickly gathered fame among the common people. In his young life as mortal man he regarded both worlds filled with lights of love and he used his passion from these feelings to unite man in a greater love bond relationship to God and each other. He was consummated by that thought. His love and passion was contagious.

The words from Yeshua rose above all others. He was the epitome of Love. In his father's heart he was courageous. In his mother's heart he was hope. To his brothers and sisters, he was pure Love. To all of us who love Yeshua, regarding his words, we began to fill our House with Love. The hurting people were a love for him.

As his reputation increased he began to work through Simon and me. We became his power to use as an extension of himself to help others. In learning the ways of my brother, Simon and I stayed within our commune for many years until Simon had to travel in Yeshua's behalf. I stayed doing the work of Yeshua by incorporating his wisdom into my daily prayers and in my temple/church I preached all he spoke of. We were popular in our Essene commune and with some of the non-Hebrews that we allowed to complete their feelings with Yeshua. These outcasts were all welcomed into my church. I was able to gather their hearts by giving them my brother's words and sharing the gift of God and healing.

Our church was gifted. In the old days we spoke of guides as a gift from God. My brother accepted this. I learned to do the same. The guides began to listen to our House, and they worked hard to help us for our tomorrows. A hard road lay ahead and we all knew our mortal lives were coming to an end. These guides prepared us intellectually for the completion of Love.

We had angels near and guides from that angelic realm. The flowers that bloom around my House are collected by people. These were the gifts from the guides. My House (the church) was the biggest place of worship for poor people.

My House has been open to anyone who wanted to feel Yeshua. I created the flame to praise him in a way that was filled with love, honor and respect. It was my temple/church that was the first ever to excite the non-Hebrews to gather and feel the perfect life and love of Yeshua.

Our church was gifted. Our home became a House filled with love directed by Yeshua. My hand is in my House for all eternity. My past lives existed in the church. I bring the thinking of my life from the power of the contact with Yeshua. I, James, remember all my lives and remain in my old House with Yeshua. I am a collective form of Hebrew and Catholic. And I choose to dwell in my Father's House in the Light of Yeshua.

My Father's House is filled with matters of Lights and Love. Those of us who dwell in it can overhear the prayers and laments of the suffering. We hear the love and proud feelings from everyday passion. To all of you in mortal form, please be aware we hear your cries. With the politics that you create in your world you create your hell. We press you all to regard each others heart. To laugh more and be filled with Love and Compassion. As a collective connection we here send you our Love.

From this House of souls, we men and women assume our Love has been accounted for. Power is Love.

A Talking Atom

An Aspect of Eileen J. Garrett

Eileen talked about atoms—particles of matter that continue after our bodies die. She described atoms as having substance. They are made up of thought that results in feeling words for communication.

An atom of mine is capable of contacting you.

These atoms are for entities who want to communicate. Our people here may choose to work with mortals. When doing so it becomes a dependency upon the mind of the medium. We must rely on the words available from the medium's vocabulary. When progress is made between both beings, then we can use more from our atoms of thought to create our independent style of expressed words for thought. When our carefully placed thoughts become interactive with people, the connected force of power results in communication.

Feelings of people remind us of what we had and we remember to remind ourselves to roll with their feelings. This connected force of power is Love. To remain hoping to speak, is a power that we use when accepting a medium. Turning over the formal thought of words is easy to do. When I feel power to use in my hand I accept the tale of that life. We here create the higher thoughts about Love. My intellectual formal thought on proving me is in the heart of man. In regard to man seeking proof he must result in Love.

For the people seeking concrete proof, it is an accident of an examination of a medium that will result in a milestone.

Appendix C

Client Interviews

> Who knows if it was Chuang Tzu dreaming a butter-
> fly, or a butterfly dreaming Chuang Tzu?
> —Chuang Tzu (369–268 BCE)

THE TRANSCRIPTS OF our interviews with Marilyn's clients are too long to be completely recorded in this book. Below are extracts from the most representative ones.

Doris Hochheiser, Florida

The first time I met Marilyn was very much meant to be. I am a very organized person who likes to plan ahead and have things in order. My daughter and family were coming to visit me from the west coast of Florida when I realized that I hadn't bought the special soy milk that our grandchildren like. Since I had to go further than the local store, I was very worried that I wouldn't be back in time to let them in since my husband wasn't coming home until later. As I passed the Holiday Inn I noticed a sign that said "Psychic Fair," and I thought, "Too

249

bad I don't have enough time—I would love to find a good psychic for my spiritual club." Then something told me to stop and I did. I went inside but it didn't seem like much of a show because there were so few psychics attending. They were all inside their booths doing their readings. Sharon[1] was sitting at a desk when I noticed Marilyn's flyer. Since I am artistic, the beautiful angel on it caught my eye and I questioned Sharon about Marilyn's talents. At that point in my life I was very suspicious of frauds. Sharon answered my questions easily and then looked me in the eye and said, "She's the real thing." There was something about her words that sent a current through my body and made the hair on my arms stand up. Now I understand that this is the body's signal when hearing the truth. Sharon invited me to the séances that Marilyn was holding that Saturday night.

I convinced my friend Barbara to go with me to the séances and that evening was the first time I met Marilyn and saw her do a "platform reading." There were about fifteen people in the room who were claiming various names that came up as Marilyn said them. Since I was a skeptic, I was trying to figure it all out when Marilyn said the name "Ann? Annie? You never noticed jewelry." My heart seemed to stop beating and I just froze and couldn't speak at all. Since no one claimed this name, Marilyn went on to bring in other names. To this day I regret not claiming Ann, my friend who had passed a few years before this event. I later remembered that she loved women's jewelry and would comment on their details. As a younger person I never noticed jewelry—I liked to look at someone's eyes or hair. One time Ann teased me when I missed noticing a very large diamond ring that one woman was wearing.

---

[1]Sharon McConnell, a friend of Marilyn's, was helping Marilyn organize events at that time.

A short time after that missed opportunity, Marilyn said, "I have Paul here." Not wanting to miss another one, I quickly raised my hand and said, "I knew a Paul." She said, "Work, work, work—all you ever do is work." I was sitting there, an older woman looking obviously like a retiree so I didn't think she was guessing about my working now. I was working when Paul died and so he never saw me retired. He was my husband's friend, a schoolteacher with afternoons off, while I worked in a commercial real estate firm for many long hours. He would often tease me about working so hard and so that night I became a believer.

My friend Barbara also became a believer when Marilyn said her father's name. Barbara acknowledged the name and then Marilyn said, "This is your *other* father, not your biological father." He was her stepfather and neither Marilyn nor I had any knowledge of this part of Barbara's past. Marilyn said that on Barbara's twelfth birthday her stepfather did something very special for her, going very much out of his way that he now wanted to acknowledge. Barbara later recalled that on her twelfth birthday her stepfather bought a bicycle in New York City and didn't want to ride it home himself before Barbara herself was able to use it so he walked it home to Brooklyn, over a bridge for many miles so that she would be the first to ride her new bike.

That night I watched and listened and validated information heard in other readings of complete strangers in the group. A young girl's father came through and Marilyn said to her, "Your father says, 'Thank you for taking care of me when I wasn't able to communicate to you during those last few years of my life. I want you to know that I understood everything you were saying.'" At the end of the séances I felt drawn to ask this girl exactly what her father's words meant, and she said, "My father wasn't able to communicate to me during the last two years of his life since he had Alzheimer's." This really shocked and comforted me at the same time because what I learned then was that not only could a soul come through after they had passed over but that a soul could still hear what their loved ones were saying in life even though a disease like Alzheimer's made a person appear they couldn't hear or comprehend.

I was so enthused with what I had learned that I scheduled a private reading with Marilyn on the phone. She scanned my body and told me that I was hypoglycemic, which I already knew. She also said that I had a thyroid problem, which I didn't know at that time. I later confirmed this with a doctor.

Marilyn then asked, "Do you have a boat?" I said, "No." Then she said, "Do you have anything to do with ships?" I again said, "No." Then she said, "I don't understand this—they're showing me a galley of a ship." I started to laugh and said, "I have an uncle Gally who has died." She said, "That's a name?" I explained that my uncle Gally's real name was Irving Galitzer but everyone called him Gally. She said, "Well, he's here now." Then Mae came through, whom I acknowledged. She told me Abe was with Mae. I said, "Good—they were married to each other." They are relatives of Gally.

She said that my daughter was in a health field and had moved far away from me. My daughter is a psychotherapist and had just moved to the west coast of Florida. She said that a close relative of mine had a new position because he replaced someone who had a breakdown. This relative had replaced a professional who was ill with a drug problem and who had a mental breakdown.

When I asked about my son Jeff, Marilyn said, "Is this a second marriage for you?" I said, "No." She said, "I don't understand this—I don't see a connection between Jeff, your husband, and you." I laughed and said, "Well, that's because Jeff was adopted by us when he was a baby." She said, "I didn't even think of that." Then she said that Jeff would be taking a test. I couldn't understand that because Jeff had finished school years before and was working in a retail store. Within two weeks he told me that they had taught him a new computer program at work and that his supervisor had sat with him to make sure he had learned this program properly. I asked Jeff, "Was it like a test?" He said, "Yes." I never anticipated that kind of a test. Marilyn also said that Jeff would have his own business, which at that point in his life seemed far-fetched because he was so happy in his job. As it turned out, on his days off, Jeff buys merchandise to sell at a flea market and makes a nice amount of money doing it. Marilyn was right about him having his own business even though it took about one year.

My cousin Deborah, who lives in the state of Washington, came to Florida and scheduled a phone reading with Marilyn. Marilyn had no idea that she was my cousin. Deborah has a sister who is about seventeen years older. During her reading different people's names came up which Deborah didn't understand. When Marilyn said, "I'm getting the name Goddard—does that mean anything to you?" Deborah said, "No." When she talked to her older sister some time afterward, her sister confirmed that the strange names that Deborah couldn't identify belonged to many of the friends and their children that her parents knew at a bungalow colony many years before. Her older sister also told her that her mother, who would now be about one hundred years old if she were alive, only wore Goddard bras that she was proud to say were rated as the best. Deborah wasn't able to understand all these messages, but her older sister validated them for her.

I brought Marilyn to our spiritual awareness club's meeting with twenty women attending her open (platform) readings. Carol was of our new members and had joined because as she got older she found that she wanted to believe in life after death more and needed proof. She sat next to me when Marilyn walked over to her and said, "Do you know Alan?" "Yes," she said, "Alan was my brother." "Has he passed?" "Yes." "Alan wants to know why you scream his name when you pray for him?" This seemed strange. When I questioned Carol afterward, she said, "Doris, Alan died suddenly, and I was so upset that when I think about him I scream as loud as I can, 'Alan!'" Then Marilyn said to her, "Who is Bianca?" Carol gripped my hand with such a force that it left a mark. I though it must be bleeding when she answered, "That's my granddaughter." Marilyn told her that Sarah Bernhardt, the deceased actress,[2] said that Bianca was very theatrical and that Carol should encourage her to continue in that profession. Carol confirmed that seven-year-old Bianca, here on earth, was indeed talented and had already performed in many plays.

I also brought my cousin Arline to our group for the first time during one of Marilyn's readings. Marilyn came to her and said, "I have Lillian here. No, wait. She wants to be called Lil-Anne." Arline squeezed my hand hard and gasped as Marilyn said, "And she has the baby with her." "And who is David?" Arline's son David's wife had given birth to twin girls prematurely several years back. The first baby girl took one breath and passed on. They still mourned this child. The other twin girl weighed only 1 lb. 1 oz. and thankfully survived beautifully. Now Arline knew that the first child was with her grand-

---

[2]Sarah Bernhardt (1844–1923) was a French stage actress. She earned the title "The Divine Sarah" and may have been the most famous actress of the nineteenth century.

mother in a safe place. Marilyn also told Arline, "Your mother is sorry she didn't let you go to college because she knows now how important it was to you." Arline went back to school and completed her degree on her own as an adult.

My friend Carrie was originally from Boston where her father was ailing in a nursing home. At another club's meeting, Marilyn was channeling Eileen and each of us was allowed to ask her a question. Carrie asked how her father was doing since he was so far away. Marilyn answered, "They are taking good care of him." Carrie was puzzled and didn't know if Marilyn meant that her father was in a hospital or a nursing home with private care. She was concerned. The doorbell rang while Marilyn was still in this channeled state and everyone's attention went to the door and then to the hostess who led in Carrie's husband who was obviously upset. He walked across the room to Carrie and whispered something in her ear, and Carrie jumped up and said, "I have to go" and they left abruptly. This created quite a commotion but since I was responsible for the group and curious about Marilyn's reaction, I focused in on her. Marilyn didn't blink or miss a beat but kept on talking. I could see that she didn't know what was going on around her and was not conscious of Carrie's hurried exit. This was the best test ever. We later found out that Carrie's dad had already died while we were all at this reading but her husband didn't want to upset her because of their long flight back to Boston. Later Carrie was comforted to know that her father was being taken good care of on the other side.

Eight months after my father had passed, I had a private reading with Marilyn face-to-face. She said, "I have your father here and he is sorry that he didn't allow you to sing and dance—you loved it so." That was so true. When I was about seven years old, my family moved to a new neighborhood, which was accessible by car. I had been scheduled to solo in a tap dance recital but my parents refused to take me back to the old neighborhood for this recital. I was hurt and angry and that stayed with me for many years but we never talked about it. Through Marilyn my father was asking forgiveness, which I easily gave him and that helped me lift a very heavy burden from my heart.

ᕯ ᕯ ᕯ

I was asked to teach a spiritual awareness workshop[3] and I told the women in my group about Marilyn's talents. They were interested in attending an open reading so I arranged one and announced the future date during one of my workshops. One woman named Linda took me aside and said, "I'm not coming. I hated my mother when she was alive so I certainly don't want to talk to her now that she's dead." She seemed so angry and unhappy that I didn't want to push her into coming, so I said, "That's fine with me—this was for your benefit. If you change your mind, just let me know." A few days later she called to say she wanted to come. At the reading Marilyn said to her, "Your mother is here and she's apologizing that she wasn't very nice to you—she just wanted to toughen you up. She's also sorry that you were one of the last." Linda gasped. Then Marilyn went to someone else on the other side of the room. A short while later she came back to Linda and again said, "She's still here and wants you to forgive her!" Linda cried along with everyone else in that room. I bumped into Linda a few weeks later and she was smiling and looked so peaceful. I had never seen her smile before. I was shocked to see such a physical change in her and told her how relaxed she looked. She said,

---

[3]Doris teaches spiritual awareness in the Wycliffe's Study Group of the Brandeis University National Women's Committee, a fund-raiser for Brandeis University.

"Doris, this thing with Marilyn has changed my life. I was the fifth child in a family of six and I realize now that it was just too much for my mother to handle. I'm not angry anymore. What a burden to take off!"

There was another lady, Ann, who I knew was widowed but didn't know anything more about her. I never give Marilyn any information except the name of the hostess. Marilyn told Ann, "I have Jesse here and he says that he wasn't so good to you and he is very proud of how far you've come through these hard times." Ann told me later that her husband was very controlling and kept her down and she went through a tough emotional time after he passed. She was very excited about this reading and told her children, who were very skeptical and thought their mother was being taken advantage of. She also told her psychiatrist, who said, "Ann, there are so many charlatans that prey on old people—I wouldn't want you hurt." Ann lost confidence and was confused and told me what everyone had said. I told her, "There are a lot of professionals who would believe your story. My daughter is a psychotherapist and she believes in the afterlife and she wouldn't tell you not to trust what you heard." I asked Ann, "What do you really believe happened?" Ann said, "I know it was him, I believe that." I said, "That's all you need to know—don't bother trying to convince anyone else—they're just not ready to absorb what you heard." Some time afterward Ann switched her therapist to a clinical psychologist who believes her story and has helped her greatly.

Susan was really a skeptic and only came to my workshop out of curiosity. She also came to one of Marilyn's open readings. Right away Rose came through and Susan raised her hand and said, "I have an Aunt Rose." But she thought to herself, "Big deal, everyone here must have an Aunt Rose who died—good guess." When Marilyn said, "Norman is here with Rose," Susan's interest grew. Norman was Aunt Rose's son who had also died. During the intermission, Susan was outside with others when Marilyn said to her, "Who is Asher? Usher? Oscar?" Susan said that Oscar was her father and he had died. Marilyn said, "He wants to let you know your mother is doing fine, she's with her family here, but we're on opposite sides of the street." Susan almost fainted. No one in that room could have known that during her parents' stormy marriage her mother would often threaten her father with, "I'm telling you now—I don't know which one of us will die first, but if you're there and you see me—cross over to the other side of the street!"

I've learned that when you believe that your life is a continuum, the small, petty things that happen don't mean very much and won't upset you. When you see the bigger picture and know that you are here for a reason, it's easier to be more relaxed with whatever happens and not to be afraid of what might happen. I've learned how to be more loving and accepting with my friends and family. I try and be less judgmental with others because I've learned that once we pass over we will understand what we've done wrong in this life. I try and forgive someone now while we share this time on earth.

Sharon McConnell, Florida

The first time I met Marilyn, she said to me, "I see clocks all around you." I thought it was a peculiar way of opening a reading. She said, "No, no, no. I see a big tall man, and you always try to make him on time." I started to laugh. She said, "I see music and lots of people around you. But that's not what you do for your job. Is it?" I said, "No, it's what I want to do." She said, "I see a letter, a big 'W'—is this someone in the entertainment business?" I said, "Yes." She said, "Could you tell me what it means?" I said, "Absolutely!" I tried to keep this man on time for all of the events I put together for him. To me he was a very prominent entertainer. It was Wayne Newton. You know, she had come that far forward.

She was one of the few that could pick out something that no one else could pick out. The people I talk to come from all over the world. The one that I think hit me the hardest was the lady whose daughter had passed in the Twin Towers. The lady told me nothing, and Marilyn came through with the jewelry her daughter had on, her name, the people she was with, how it happened, the fact she spoke with her dad on the cell phone. The woman called me, and I don't think there are words that can describe her gratitude and closure the woman received from Marilyn's reading.

On the fourth of July, it was my husband's sixtieth birthday. I prepared fireworks, hired a DJ, and invited forty or fifty people, including Marilyn, to my house. During the party, my brother-in-law Vinny walked up and sang a song, which was the favorite song of his late wife and my late sister, Valerie. Marilyn was in the house talking to friends when he started to sing. The next minute people were looking at her very strangely, which prompted me to look to see lights around the pool and everything [to make sure everything was working properly].

I looked at Marilyn and I noticed that her facial expression had changed. I realized that she was in trance. She was crying. Then she started to speak to me as Eileen. Eileen spoke with an Irish accent and that's why people around us couldn't understand: "Who is this person talking with a brogue?" But she was calling me like she was my sister, who had died about a year ago. There was no doubt in my mind. I had heard

Eileen speak through so that I knew it was Eileen. Eileen was relaying a message from my sister through Marilyn.

She was telling me, "Thank you, my sister dear, you've been so good to me, and I am glad that you brought my family together." I started to talk to her as Eileen to bring her out of this trance, to bring her back to the reality without touching her. I kept referring to Eileen, "Eileen, remember where we are—We are at a party. It's a happy time. Tell Val that we all love her. We are glad that she is here with us."

Marilyn's face relaxed and I realized she was coming back to us. She looked around, and she said, "How did I get here?"

Joyce Oates, Michigan

It's been close to six or seven years. And actually when I first talked to her I had never met her.

A friend of mine was employed at the airport, and I used to be with the airline. And this woman was not a close friend and didn't know anything of me other than we saw each other quite a bit when I would come through there because my children lived there. We both were very interested in psychics so she told me that I should call Marilyn. She said she's just wonderful. She gave me her number. I waited maybe a couple of months when I really had this terrible drive to call her. So I called and she really astounded me.

Marilyn said to me, "There is a man coming." My first thought was it's my husband because I am a widow. I said this to her. She said, "Well, he calls you Monkey." I just started crying immediately. This was my father's nickname for me. He called me that all of my life. And it was a very private thing; it wasn't something that everybody knew. And even my children didn't know it. I couldn't believe it.

The things my father said (through Marilyn) were really

true. He apologized for my childhood, which was not a really nice one, although I think I was kind of created to be able to handle things.

My mother was a hard person. She and I would really disagree quite a bit. I used to tell her, "Mother, life is about love and you have to love everyone." And my mother didn't love anybody, really. She never even showed love toward her family. This was something that nobody knew. In the reading, Marilyn said, "There's a woman coming." And then she said, "Her message to you is, 'You were right, Joyce, it's all about love.'" I was just crying and crying. I just couldn't believe it. My mother found that out when she went to heaven.

Then my father said, "Why did you quit writing? You should go back to writing. You were very good at it." I only do it occasionally. And it just comes to me at odd times and I'll just write poetry. Nobody else knew this, either. It's a book that I just keep here at home. And my father had no idea that I was doing this. I never did it until after he had passed away.

I met Marilyn probably two or three years after I first talked with her. I've never met anybody quite like her. She's so kind. We talked for about an hour and I wanted to pay her. She refused to take money from me. It's like we've always known one another. I really have a deep love for her and I think she has a love for me.

My son Steven passed away with a heart attack almost three years ago. We had disagreements. I would call him and he would not talk or he would simply say, "Mom, I've got to go." I would tell him that I loved him, but Steven would not say anything. He died before we ever made amends. When Steven came through, he kept saying all the way through the conversation how much he loved me and he was so sorry that he had not called me.

Steven had a friend named Eddie who had been killed in an automobile accident five years before Steven passed away. There was no way for Marilyn to know that my son's best friend was named Eddie. My son came through and said that Eddie was there with him and that Eddie had a bike. When she said that, I asked, "A bike?" And she said, "Yeah. Evidently, Eddie always wanted to ride a bike in heaven." And she said, "Your son and Eddie are singing 'Bad boys, Bad boys.' He says, 'Tell Pat that Eddie is with me.'"

I couldn't think for the life of me who Pat was. Two or three months later, all of a sudden, in the middle of the night, I woke up knowing who Pat was—Pat was Eddie's mother. I called Eddie's brother. He said, "Oh my God, Eddie used to have a motorcycle." I never knew Eddie had a motorcycle. I told him to tell this to his mother. He would know how to tell her.

Oh, there was another thing my son said to me. I asked him, "When it's my turn to go, will you come get me?" And here's the jokester again. He said, "Do you want me to come as a little boy or as a man?" I said, "As a man." I know that when I go, he'll be the one who comes to take me home.[4]

Tracey Richmond, New Jersey

From the moment I first talked to Marilyn, I felt comfortable. I didn't feel like I was being taken or that this was a joke. I was a little skeptical about it but she was very smooth talking, very calming, not asking me questions like "Is that right? Is that right?" She was just going with the flow. She talked very slow. I'll never forget what really turned me on to her was one of the things she first said to me.

She said, "You have a guardian angel and her name starts

---

[4]Joyce passed away in 2004.

with an A. She is an older woman. I believe her name is Angel or Andrea or Angie." Angela was my grandmother's name. As soon as she said that to me, I felt so wonderful knowing that throughout the whole thing. She was saying things about my grandmother that nobody would know, not even if you looked the stuff up on the Internet or did a background check. There is no way. There are nicknames she would call me. From that moment, I was just so into listening to what she said. Everything she said to me has come true one way or another. Everything. It is amazing.

Marilyn mentioned about a trip to Atlantic City with my grandmother. My grandmother was like a second mother to me. When my grandmother was at the end of her time, we made a yearly trip to Atlantic City to see the Ice Capades.[5] When we were getting ready to leave the hotel to go to the show, my grandma became very ill. I was so upset because I wanted to go to the show. She wanted to make me happy so she went, still. She had to be rushed in an ambulance to the hospital because she fell at the show. I was only little and didn't realize how much she suffered from leukemia, and I wanted my way. She did it for me. I look back now and know I was selfish, but when you're a child, you just want your way, and that's it.

When I was eighteen years old, unfortunately I got pregnant and had an abortion. Nobody really knew that except me and my boyfriend. Marilyn said to me, "Do you have children?" I said, "No, I want to someday, but, no." She said, "I see a little girl. Your grandmother is holding a child. Your grandmother is telling me she is your child." I said, "What?" She said, "Were you ever pregnant?" I said, "Yes." She said, "That's your baby." It was a girl. How would Marilyn know that?

She is a normal person. She has some amazing gift and she

---

[5]The Ice Capades was a traveling ice-skating show.

uses it for good, which is a rare find nowadays. I was in awe when I met her. I was like a five-year-old girl looking for some candy in the candy jar. I really became a kinder person and I thank her for that.

Diane, Florida

A year and a half after my husband, John, passed, I called Marilyn in 2003. She immediately felt the name John and said, "He wants you to get rid of his shoes."

Hearing that, I was moved. John couldn't have cared less about clothes, but he liked one pair of moccasins that he wore all the time. He'd resewn them, and they were beaten all up. That's what he had on his feet every time he walked out of the door. I couldn't get rid of his shoes. They sat in the closet and they were still there. After his death, when I needed to feel him close, I'd stand in his shoes in my walk-in closet. John was six feet seven and I am six feet one inches tall. I have big feet and his shoes were even bigger on me. But I just wanted to bring him closer and feel his warmth and love.

Marilyn said these exact words, "He's telling you to get rid of his shoes. *No one can fill his shoes.*" This is so John. It's not like she said a general thing like he wants you to get rid of his clothes and move on.

In the middle of the phone call, Marilyn told me, "John wants you to read a poem, 'A Boob and Adam.'"

I asked, "How do you spell that?"

Marilyn said, "I don't know. I am just hearing it."

So I jotted down "A Boob and Adam." That was how it sounded to me.

As soon as I got off the phone with Marilyn, I e-mailed a friend of John's in New England. He is a book dealer and does a little writing. I wrote, "Sounds crazy. I am trying to find out this poem. Sounds like 'A Boob and Adam'?" I did not hear anything back from him.

The next morning I woke up. I sat in bed and thought, "I have got to find out what Marilyn was talking about."

I fumbled through the whole house, then entered John's study room and searched in the shelf in the room. On this shelf there was a toy sailboat made for John by his grandfather. Beside that little childhood treasure, I had put John's ashes and a picture of John in front of it. And a funeral pamphlet of a barely known acquaintance who had died of cancer in 1999 was sitting between the ashes and John's picture. I reached to the pamphlet and turned it around. I almost passed out. At that point, I felt as if I had won the lottery. On the back of the pamphlet, there was a short poem.

Abou Ben Adhem

Abou Ben Adhem (may his tribe increase!)
Awoke one night from a deep dream of peace,
And saw, within the moonlight in his room,
Making it rich, and like a lily in bloom,
An angel writing in a book of gold.

Exceeding peace had made Ben Adhem bold,
And to the Presence in the room he said,
"What writest thou?" The vision rais'd its head,
And with a look made of all sweet accord,
Answer'd, "The names of those who love the Lord."

"And is mine one?" said Abou. "Nay, not so,"
Replied the angel. Abou spoke more low,
But cheerily still; and said, "I pray thee, then,
Write me as one that loves his fellow men."

The angel wrote, and vanish'd. The next night
It came again with a great wakening light,

And show'd the names whom love of God had blest,
And lo! Ben Adhem's name led all the rest.

—James Leigh Hunt

John must have used this idea to report that he wanted to do the right thing and be a good person. To him, that was the most important thing. I am comforted to know that John used his own way to let me know that he is there. He exists.

Before John passed away, he insisted that our daughter, Polly, have the best education possible and enter the best college possible. After he passed, I was not on track at all. All she cared about was dancing professionally. Polly left the private school she had been attending for years. When I called Marilyn, I was homeschooling Polly. I believed the education was not enough and thought, "Oh, God, if John was watching, he would be going crazy that I am not being strict enough. I was always softer than he was."

Marilyn revealed John's updated view regarding Polly's education, without being asked: "He said that, in his physical life, if he were here, it would have made him crazy. But from where he is now, seeing from a different perspective, it is OK. And it would be a waste of money to force Polly to go to college because that's not what she is going to do. Instead, he wants her to receive good theatrical or dancing training."

With the mental support from John, I feel much less guilty about allowing Polly to follow her heart. Later Polly was admitted to a dance school in Philadelphia and did some modeling in Miami. She is in New York City to pursue acting.

Jacqueline, Florida

When I talked to Marilyn the first time, I had hoped my mother would come through, but she did not. Instead, Marilyn said,

"Gary is here. He says he is your husband."

I thought, "Oh, no, he will not leave me alone even though he is on the other side now." But I just said reluctantly, "Yes."

"He wants to apologize to you for mistreating you throughout your marriage," Marilyn said. "He thought that he was the smart one and put you down. He is saying that was a mistake."

"Is this really him? Has he changed?" I thought and did not know what to say.

Marilyn continued, "He said he did not understand your strong spiritual beliefs because they did not follow the standards set by traditional churches. Now he is able to recognize that your beliefs are valid, too. He also wants to apologize for his cruelty, Jacqueline."

Why did he apologize now all of a sudden? I was shaken in confusion and still could not say a word.

"He is saying that he never accepted the concept of death for himself. During his almost seven years of illness, the pain was very intense. The more he did not want to be separated from you, the more he did not want you to see him suffer the indignity of dying. He is explaining that he wanted and needed to distance you from what he described as the indignity of how he was dying and the changes on him.

"Throughout the years he thought that his mind and emotions were functioning well, but on crossing over, he realized that he had not been balanced mentally or emotionally. He was not able to stabilize his behavior toward you. He now recognizes that he was not functioning in a loving and a rational way—his mind was unable to function effectively, even though he did not know it at that time."

I finally understood why the more ill Gary became, the more estranged and hostile he was towards me. I felt as if my late husband's blue eyes were twinkling at me with dizzying openness and mischievous affection.

While my mind was occupied with these thoughts, Marilyn asked, "Do you have a daughter?"

"No."

"Well, your husband says she is with him. And he calls her Our Little Miscarriage. Your husband is saying that Our Little Miscarriage will reincarnate as your granddaughter. She will have red hair, too."

This is amazing! Marilyn did not know Gary had red hair at all, and I did not tell her that Gary had been devastated over my ectopic pregnancy before our son was born.

Bibliography

Cass, V. B. (1986). Female healers in the Ming and the lodge of ritual and ceremony. *Journal of the American Oriental Society 106*(1), 233–245.

Fuller, J. G. (1978). *Airmen Who Would Not Die.* New York: Putnam.

Garrett, E. J. (1945). *Telepathy, In Search of a Lost Faculty.* New York: Creative Age.

Garrett, E. J. (1968). *Many Voices, The Autobiography of a Medium.* New York: G. P. Putnam's Sons.

Garrett, E. J. (2002). *Adventures in the Supernormal.* New York: Helix.

Hotchner, A. E. (1966). *Papa Hemingway: A Personal Memoir.* New York: Random House.

Index